"Anyone who is acquainted with t
here will not only revisit the facts as
with the author about what thoughts might have gone through the
twisted mind of the perpetrator—both perspectives in keeping with
the rich potential of 'faction.' Those familiar with   Capote's *In
Cold Blood*   ..n masterful
and will con   pote has nothing on Cawelti. All readers should
steel themselv   .: a disturbing encounter with the bafflements of a
brother's com   on of a horrific act and an unpardonable sin.

—Robert '   sh, author, *West Bound: Stories of Providence*

"The Marks were an Iowa farming family less well-known than the
Clutters of Kansas, but comparable in the hideousness of their murders. Using interviews and trial transcripts, Scott Cawelti has given us
the terse and mercifully distanced account of how one jealous brother
carried out the crime. The allusion to Cain and Abel is apt; one dearly
wishes the killer had read that story, and learned its lesson."

—Robley Wilson, author, *The Victim's Daughter*

"The happy story of the family farm, father and sons laboring together
in the fields glad of one another's company, masks an ugly truth. There
is money in the land. There is jealousy between brothers, and fathers
have favorites. In *Brother's Blood*, Scott Cawelti pries his fingers into the
horrible wound that can result and shows us that awful truth."

—J. Harley McIlrath, author, *Possum Trot*

"I still recall the fear of that Halloween weekend when a mass murderer
stalked our town. Scott Cawelti painstakingly brings together all the
material to answer the questions that still haunt us regarding this brutal
tragedy, and even takes the risk of entering the murderer's mind."

—Barbara Lounsberry, author, *Time and Chance*

"*Brother's Blood* is a thoroughly researched and straightforward account of a horrific crime. Scott Cawelti has captured the darkest of deeds—the cold-blooded and premeditated murder of family members. Reminiscent of true crime classics like *In Cold Blood* and *Fatal Vision*, *Brother's Blood* is absorbing, tense, and disturbing. Scott Cawelti's well-researched and taut narrative will keep readers turning the pages."

—Thomas Wolf, co-author, *Midnight Assassin: A Murder in America's Heartland*

"Read this book? Sure. Just don't plan on sleeping anytime soon. Scott Cawelti rejuvenates the crime procedural by imagining his way fully into the heart of a promising classmate—and convicted killer—and elevates the form by inviting us on a dark, harrowing ride. In the book's heartbreaking coda, we interrogate Cawelti's sources directly. And this, I'm convinced, is what makes *Brother's Blood* such an engrossing read. A lifelong essayist, Cawelti knows how to include the reader in a conversation. What makes a killer different from you and me? Something in the blood? Mere circumstance? Cawelti has ideas. And so, I'm sure, will you."

— John Bresland, Tamarack Award Winner for Fiction, and Nonfiction Writer-in-Residence, Northwestern University

"A provocative work of creative nonfiction that includes some wonderful leaps of imaginative fiction (revolving around motivations, dreams, and trenchant dialogue) to tell its story of betrayal and murder. Cawelti's Jerry Mark is a borderline sociopath, his dreams revealing a cold, cold heart, and like James M. Cain's Walter Neff he's a smart-talking character who's not quite as smart as he thinks he is. Genuinely creepy and compelling."

—Grant Tracey, editor, *North American Review* and author, *Lovers & Strangers*

BROTHER'S BLOOD

a heartland Cain and Abel

SCOTT CAWELTI

ICE CUBE PRESS
NORTH LIBERTY, IOWA

Brother's Blood: A Heartland Cain and Abel

ISBN 9781888160598   3 5 7 9 8 6 4 2 (second printing, 10/2011)

Library of Congress Control Number: 2011926077

Ice Cube Press, LLC
205 N. Front St.
North Liberty, Ia 52317

The paper used in this publication meets the minimum requirements of the American National Standard for Information Sciences—Permanence of Paper for Printed Library Materials, ANSI Z39.48-1992

Manufactured in the United States of America

Disclaimer: (also found on pg. 151.): BROTHER'S BLOOD is primarily a nonfiction story, with interludes of fictional recreation of conversations, personal thoughts and dreams. As a nonfiction story, readers may appreciate knowing my sources. I offer them unedited except for elisions and original errors marked "sic," letting them stand on their own as information readers can use to form their own decisions as to the accuracy of the story.

I had no access to sources for family conversations, dreams, or thoughts of any of the people. Those details I fictionalized in order to create a readable and engaging narrative. My fictionalized account may be close to the truth, but this remains a mystery as I do not and could not have known what literally occurred. However, all events, places, people, and place names are based on fact. From my experience even those who experienced the events have differing memories, so the past always remains ambiguous—part fact, part imagined fiction.

I trust readers will understand the need for poetic license, even when real people are involved, in order to create a story from what is essentially a series of reports, transcripts, newspaper stories, and interviews—the raw material on which I drew. In other words, connections to real persons, living and dead, is intended throughout, though tentative at times due to the inevitable gulf between third person observing and first person knowledge, or an absence of factual material upon which to draw.

Dedicated to my wife Angeleita Floyd, whose good humor, intelligence, and passion for life seem unbounded, and to my children Christa and Jason, to whom I am ever grateful for teaching their dad so many life lessons.

TABLE OF CONTENTS

Foreword

TWO WORDS. That's all it took to transform the discovery of the deaths of four members of a rural Iowa farm family into a multiple-murder mystery that has mesmerized a community and mystified it even to this day.

"No gun." Black Hawk County Deputy Sheriff Mike Kubik appeared near shock as he uttered those words when he stepped out to the back porch of the Leslie Mark farm home on that sunny, warm Nov. 1, 1975 morning. Those of us clustered at the foot of the steps to the porch suspected a far different finding. It had seemed likely that a member of the family—most likely the husband/father—in a fit of uncontrollable rage had used a gun to slay his pretty young wife, their two small children and finally, himself. The weapon, we assumed, would be found under the man's body.

With that theory gone we had was a mass slaying that, news wise, was reminiscent of the infamous Clutter family slaying in rural Kansas a few years earlier.

Alerted by a message on a police radio, another reporter and I had arrived at the Mark farm less than an hour after the bodies had been discovered by Leslie Mark's parents the morning after Halloween. As we walked to the house we saw a man leaning against a windmill, staring at the ground. We asked what was going on. "They're all dead," he said, repeatedly. Who? "All of them; the Marks," replied Clark Renner, farmer and friend of the Mark family.

We were to learn that the only people in the house at that time were the victims, the Mark parents and a deputy sheriff. My reporter friend and I were the fifth and sixth people to arrive on the scene. From then on, I was married to this story. One of my last assignments before retiring in January 1996 after 28 years as a *Des Moines Register* reporter was to cover another "Mark Case" court proceeding, one of several that followed the crime that by then was more than 20 years old.

Often I have characterized the Mark Case as "a story that never dies." I attest to that by the regular inquiries I continue to receive about my work on the story and my opinions on the outcome. No other event that I covered in more than forty years as a journalist, including more than 100 murder cases, has elicited as much public interest.

In *Brother's Blood*, Scott Cawelti accurately documents the events of years preceding the Mark killings and the years to follow, while employing some creative license in key episodes. It's a compelling account of one of Iowa's most sensational crimes.

The reader will be taken into the life of a brother of the slain Leslie Mark, as well as some of his presumed thoughts and motivations. From personal experience I concluded that Jerry Mark was a person of contrasting and unpredictable personalities. In my few direct contacts with him I found him sometimes to be pleasant, polite, almost charming. On other occasions, he treated me with obstinacy and intense dislike, never bothering to explain why.

To this day, Jerry Mark has a following of loyal friends who have defended him from the beginning of this horrible crime. They are people who grew up with him, were neighbors or schoolmates and, as one often told me, people who said simply "we have faith in Jerry."

Then, there are those who think otherwise, and it is this split that has engendered doubt, confusion, and questions within the Cedar Falls-Waterloo community. In my extended career reporting on Iowa murders and other crimes I never covered one that ripped into a city, county, or even a state as the case of the Mark murders.

Cawelti's account explores all angles of the case, leaving little doubt about the truth of the ultimate outcome.

Jack Hovelson
Des Moines Register Staff Writer, retired

Jack Hovelson was born in Osage, Iowa, in 1932, and graduated from the University of Northern Iowa in 1957 with a degree in Social Science, Journalism, and English. He wrote for the Fort Dodge *Messenger* from 1959-60, then the Waterloo *Courier* as Assistant City Editor from 1960-1968. He was hired by the *Des Moines Register* as a staff writer in 1968, and became the *Register*'s one-man Waterloo bureau. He worked in that position until he retired in 1996.

Foreword Two

IN THE LIFE OF an agent, there is always that one case that stands out. For me, this case began on November 2, 1975 in Cedar Falls, Iowa. I was a newly assigned supervising agent for the Bureau of Criminal Investigation. I had worked with Dave Dutton, Black Hawk County Attorney, for the previous five years and we had formed a friendship and successful working relationship. Together again, we found ourselves walking up to the Mark family farm that morning to review the crime scene.

The inside of the house was in disarray with drawers and rooms that had been ransacked. We noted a flower pot that had been thrown through the window down the hall. The pride and joy of the family, the grandfather clock, had also been damaged. The husband and wife were found in their beds, shot execution style. Two innocent children were found in their second floor bedrooms and had also been killed in the same manner. We observed several other abnormalities with the crime scene. After leaving the farm house, Dutton and I spoke about what we had seen. We agreed that someone had murdered an entire family as if to saw off one limb from the Mark family tree. The suspect was obviously filled with personal rage and this was simply not a robbery gone wrong as it was staged to appear.

Jerry Mark had thought that time and distance would be his insurance policy for committing the perfect crime and escaping back to California. However, he had not factored in that the State of Iowa would assemble an investigative team with experienced agents from the BCI, skilled detectives from the Waterloo Police Department and a highly qualified team of lawyers accompanying Dave Dutton. Jerry Mark would soon learn that his insurance policy had run out.

Finally, after 36 years, Scott Cawelti has produced a thorough and accurate portrayal of the events that took place in November of 1975 in a rural Iowa farm house. Through his extensive research and personal interviews, Cawelti has captured the essence of this complex investigation. The reader will walk alongside the investigators and prosecutors to relive this epic tale of jealousy and rage.

Tom Ruxlow

March, 2011

Tom Ruxlow began his career in law enforcement in 1962 as a police officer for the city of Cedar Falls, Iowa. He received promotions to the ranks of Sergeant and Lieutenant.

In 1967 he joined the Bureau of Criminal Investigation and began as a field agent working homicides and other major crimes and was promoted to Supervisor. He became the Assistant Director of all investigations and spent his last nine years as the Director of the Division of Criminal Investigation. In 1992, Tom joined Caterpillar as the Director of Global Security and Aviation Services and retired in 2004.

Tom received a business degree from the University of Northern Iowa and a Masters degree in Public Administration from Drake University in Des Moines, Iowa. Tom attended the FBI National Academy in 1975.

Tom is married to Diane, a retired school teacher and they have one daughter Rachel who is an elementary school teacher.

Preface

As I LOOK BACK on my fifty-year career as a lawyer I am struck by the unexpected events in the lives of ordinary people which put them to a test, showing how they will react and revealing their essential character. I suspect sit-com writers, modern day versions of Greek "fates" who were always testing both gods and humans, script these events.

My test, and that of others in this saga, started on a Saturday morning when I was preparing to travel to Cedar Rapids to watch my daughter participate in a district swim meet.

As I finished shaving, the phone rang. The voice of the Black Hawk County Sheriff responded to my "Hello."

"Dave, there has been a murder at the Mark farm north of Cedar Falls. It appears that we have four dead bodies." Without doubt, what followed in the ensuing months and years was the most remarkable murder investigation and trial in the history of Iowa.

Before the call came from the Sheriff that first day of November 1975, I had decided to resign my elected position as the Black Hawk County Attorney but I had not yet made my decision known. I was able to convince the Board of Supervisors to appoint David Correll, my assistant, to fill my unexpired term. I was a part-time Prosecutor and I wanted to devote full time to my work as a Civil Trial Lawyer. Since I had the most experience on the staff, I was appointed Special

Prosecutor to handle the trial. I learned later that David Correll was a law school classmate of Jerry Mark.

Not to be outdone in the "small world" realm, I came home from my law practice one evening, several years before the murder, and found Jerry Mark sitting in my living room telling members of the local League of Women Voters how to solve the social problems of the world. Jerry had been in the Peace Corps, had served in Brazil, and was working for the local Legal Aid Society. He was bright, engaging, personable, and polite.

During the first day of the investigation, the first clue found by the agents of the Iowa Bureau of Criminal Investigation was discovered in the exact same way that the murderer dropped it. As the agent was crossing the ditch to look at the former telephone junction box to see if the wires had been cut, he fell in a hole. As his hand went to the ground to break his fall, it closed on rounds of live ammunition. He picked up several .38 Long Colt cartridges manufactured by Winchester Western and sold to Jerry Mark at Ken's Sporting Goods store in Paso Robles, California, some 2,000 miles from the murder scene. We are confident that when Jerry purchased those bullets, he couldn't imagine that investigators from the "hick" state of Iowa would find him in a million years.

He grossly underestimated Tom Ruxlow of the BCI and his agents and detectives from the Waterloo Police Department who worked the case. Ruxlow assigned his agents to stop at every truck stop and restaurant from Cedar Falls, Iowa, to Jerry Mark's home in Berkeley, California, along what was believed to be the route that Mark rode on his Honda 450 motorcycle. Agents searched for employees who could identify Mark and tell the jury when and where they saw him. Even the most optimistic assessment of what that effort would produce was exceeded, which led to overwhelming, albeit circumstantial, evidence of guilt. Jerry Mark set out to commit the perfect crime, but his efforts were eclipsed by the perfect investigation conducted by Ruxlow and his team.

Due to his family's wealth and Mark's background as a lawyer, the defense hired former Iowa Attorney General Larry Scalise to defend him. Scalise was an outstanding lawyer who had successfully defended many persons accused of high profile crimes. On one occasion, Scalise gained an acquittal of a young man who was accused of killing a town marshal during a traffic stop. The young man, who was a student in a community college, was studying to become a police officer, yet had signed a confession. That is how good Larry was at his craft. I say that about Larry Scalise only to illustrate how compelling the evidence was against Jerry Mark and how it kept coming into the record.

The Mark murder case is historic in many respects including the way that circumstantial evidence was used to demonstrate how all of Mark's activities were consistent with his being the murderer and neutralized any facts which might appear to be inconsistent with his guilt. Circumstantial evidence, unlike direct evidence where someone provides eyewitness testimony of the murder, cannot show "directly" who committed the crime. It shows instead all of the evidence consistent with guilt—instrumentality and opportunity—and negates all evidence consistent with innocence or alibi.

Even great police work could not have solved this crime were it not for the perfect timing which accompanied their work. Had the subpoena for the phone records for the pay phones along I-80 been served upon the Bell System one day later, all of the millions of records from the pay phones would have been destroyed along with records of the calls made by Mark to his girlfriend as he headed toward Iowa. These records established that he was on I-80 headed for Iowa as opposed to his being in the desert attempting to "find himself" as he claimed in his statement to the police. Had Jack Makedonski, a Waterloo native, not been on duty at Ken's Sporting Goods store in Paso Robles when the investigators came by, we may not have known his Iowa connection with Mark and the greetings they exchanged when the bullets were purchased. The same can be said for all of the employees of the stores along I-80 who identified Mark at the trial.

One of the witnesses who identified Mark on his trip to Iowa to kill his brother and his brother's family was a highway patrolman from Nebraska who had just buried his young adult son. His family was at a truck stop on I-80 for a meal after the funeral and burial. As the trooper was looking wistfully out the window thinking of his dead son, he saw Jerry Mark ride up to the gas pump on his motorcycle. The trooper thought for a moment that Mark (the red headed cyclist) was his own son—another amazing and riveting moment in the unfolding evidence at the trial.

Finally, the case was blessed by the administration of justice by a brilliant trial judge, Carroll Engelkes, who diligently protected the rights of the accused while at the same time allowing the state to prove its case. Judge Engelkes commented at the conclusion of the trial that every aspect of this case was guided by the hand of the almighty. Whether or not that's true, it surely came to seem so.

In *Brother's Blood*, Scott Cawelti tells the full story of the execution-style murder of Leslie and Jorjean Mark and their two children. Cawelti brings the murder, the investigation, and trial to life in the special way that only an author who had intimate knowledge of the Mark family could. Scott was a high school classmate of Jerry's growing up and also lived for years in the same farm neighborhood as the Mark family. Truman Capote, in his landmark work of creative nonfiction, *In Cold Blood*, also claimed intimate knowledge of the killers of the Clutter family, and in some ways, the cases are similar. Cawelti also conducted extensive interviews with all the major characters, and followed it through several years before developing the narrative in its present form.

This story, along with sources, details the Mark family murders and what they came to mean for those who lived with this case for years, through the investigation, trial, and many appeals. It contains lessons for all of us, including the enduring power—and relevance—of the Biblical story of Cain and Abel. I am both grateful and thankful for Cawelti's engaging and accurate exploration of the Mark family murders in *Brother's Blood*.

David Dutton
March, 2011

David Dutton is a trial lawyer. His career began in 1960, handling tort and commercial cases. He served as prosecuting attorney for Black Hawk County from 1969 to 1975 and continued handling murder cases on a state-wide basis until 1981. His trial practice continues with a wide variety of civil and criminal cases in state and federal courts, as well as proceedings before state and local administrative bodies.

David is a Fellow in the American College of Trial Lawyers. He is listed in *The Best Lawyers in America* in Product Liability, Professional Malpractice, and Automobile Collision. He is also listed in *Chambers USA* in Business Litigation. He is the past President of the Iowa Academy of Trial Lawyers, the Iowa Chapter of ABOTA and the Iowa County Attorneys Association. He served as State Chairman of the American College of Trial Lawyers. Dave is also a member of the Iowa Association for Justice.

David is a competitive athlete in endurance sports: road races, triathlons, and swimming.

BROTHER'S BLOOD

Part I: Story

Introduction

Cain said to Abel his brother, "Let us go out to the field." And when they were in the field Cain rose up against his brother Abel, and killed him. Then the Lord said to Cain, "Where is Abel your brother?" He said, "I do not know. Am I my brother's keeper?" And the Lord said, "What have you done? The voice of your brother's blood is crying to me from the ground." —King James Version: Genesis 4: 8-10

At the end of the June 1976 trial of Jerry Mark, Special Prosecutor David Dutton referred to this Old Testament story, and from then on the case was known as the "Cain and Abel Murders." Mark was charged with murdering his brother Leslie, Leslie's wife Jorjean, and their two preschool children, Julie and Jeffrey, on Halloween night, October 31, 1975. The murders occurred at the rural Mark "homeplace" on Union Road near Finchford, about eight miles northwest of Cedar Falls, Iowa, my home town.

I knew the Mark family by reputation, and the second eldest son, Jerry, as a high school classmate. Jerry graduated in 1960, one year before me, and I often spoke to him in the Cedar Falls High hallways and at choir rehearsals—we were both singers. He was always friendly, polite, and a leader; his high school class elected him as Vice-President during his senior year.

The murders of the entire Leslie Mark family sent shockwaves not just through Cedar Falls, but all of Iowa. During the first week of November, the state's major papers carried the story as front-page news.

Iowans think of themselves as civilized, welcoming, and their state as having the lowest crime rate in the country, and therefore a great place to raise children. The brutal, calculated, execution-style murders left Midwesterners shocked and dismayed. And downright scared.

Many compared the murders to the rural Kansas slayings that Truman Capote captured in his landmark nonfiction work *In Cold Blood*, published in 1966. In that book, two drifters blundered their way into the rural Clutter family home and basically murdered the family as part of a robbery gone wrong. Those killers were sociopaths, driven by dark forces and random opportunities.

Drifters—that was the assumption, since no Iowan and certainly no local citizen would be capable of the Mark murders. So when Jerry Mark was arrested nine days after the murders, and charged with this unthinkable crime, the shock waves rattled the community as much as the murders. Not only was this brutal killer born and raised among us, he had murdered family. And he was a lawyer, a Peace Corps Volunteer—the polar opposite of a deranged drifter, and the last person any of us would have suspected.

I was literally speechless when I found out, and remained shocked for days. Jerry Mark? My success-bound high school classmate? A monster? Not possible.

There wasn't much news at first; Jerry was released on bond posted by his family. During the six-month pre-trial investigation he lived in Cedar Falls with his parents and worked at the University of Northern Iowa. Since I had been teaching at UNI since 1968, we were on the same payroll.

Though I saw Jerry occasionally on campus—he worked in the UNI administration building—I didn't speak to him. Actually I was rather afraid of him, given what he had been charged with. In fact, I had no contact with him at all until 1980, when I interviewed him in Fort Madison, site of Iowa's maximum-security prison.

He had been convicted four years earlier and, because I was so familiar with the case, the town, and particularly Mark himself, I felt driven to write about it.

After exchanging several letters, he agreed to an interview, and I met with him for a couple of hours, talking about his case. He was interested in getting me to tell his story because he thought it would help his appeals. The evidence was all circumstantial, after all, and had his defense team gotten just one juror to doubt the prosecution's sixty-some witnesses, he would be a free man. It didn't happen during the trial, and he blamed his defense team, his father, the corrupt legal system—everyone but himself.

During the summer of 1980, I (and Linda Kettner, the Cedar Falls *Record* reporter who had covered the trial for that paper) also interviewed Jerry's mother Dorothy, George and Margaret Colthurst, Jorjean's parents, prosecutor David Dutton, Iowa BCI agent Tom Ruxlow, and Lawrence Scalise, Jerry's defense attorney. I had an appointment to interview Merrilyn Forrest ("Mimi") in California, who by then was Jerry's ex-wife, but John Sandre, who had continued as Jerry's lawyer, would not permit it because more appeals were forthcoming.

I decided to wait. And wait. For three decades, Jerry kept losing appeals, but never gave up. Then in 2006, Judge Donald O'Brien of the 8th U.S. District Court ordered that Mark be released or given a new trial. O'Brien insisted that the prosecution had withheld exculpatory evidence that might have exonerated him.

For the third time, the Mark murders shocked me to my core. Suddenly Jerry Mark was back in the headlines, thirty years after his conviction. After Judge O'Brien's decision was reversed in 2007, Jerry Mark seems to have exhausted all his appeals, though he still insists, by all reports, on his innocence.

I decided I had to tell the story at last, fully and completely, beginning to end. This is that story. I've kept the facts as I found them, but created characters from real people as I knew them from interviews, experience, observations, news stories, trial transcripts, and police interviews.

My hope is that readers will learn the full truth about what happened before, during, and after that terrible night at the Mark homeplace, and will begin to understand the motives and methods used by the killer—and his probable state of mind through it all.

Scott Cawelti
April, 2011

1: Revolver

JERRY MARK TOOK a March morning to inspect the pile of decrepit camping equipment, castaway clothes, towels, small kitchen appliances, and other household debris from the Ford pickup camper. He and Mimi, his live-in girlfriend, had spirited the camper away from outside her husband Alga's mobile home near Berkeley. Alga wasn't about to let Mimi keep anything from their failing marriage, so Jerry and Mimi felt they might just take the camper and recover something of value. Alga and Mimi had registered the truck in both their names, so technically she and Jerry could not be accused of stealing.

Glancing over the mound of camping and kitchen junk they had tossed into their storage shed, Jerry saw nothing that seemed remotely valuable. With his full red-brown beard and tousled mop, he resembled a bear as he pawed and picked over the rubble: A beat-up Coleman camp stove; ancient cans of Green Giant corn, beans, and peas; a rolled-up moldy canvas pup tent; battered kitchen utensils; folded but threadbare towels, and musty toiletries. Dumpster refuse, he thought.

Jerry felt bored by the whole adventure. He and Mimi knew her marriage to Alga was essentially over, thanks to a dozen mutual incompatibilities and this last straw, her moving in with Jerry, Alga's former good friend. So Alga would never give her anything, not even stuff she owned, without a court order. He acted like a wronged teenager, alternating temper tantrums with self-pity. Not that he behaved generously even during good times, but Mimi had given up on their marriage long before Alga sensed anything amiss.

Earlier that year Alga had threatened Mimi with an old handgun, Jerry remembered, waving it in her face and scaring her witless when she wouldn't discuss their failing marriage. He wanted to negotiate, and when she wouldn't, he got the gun out and traumatized her. Jerry wasn't too surprised by Alga's violent streak. He seemed volatile and angry, and at one time mentioned the Ku Klux Klan as a group he thought had some good ideas. Jerry now wondered how they could ever have been friends.

Mimi rationalized moving the camper. She felt sure she could exchange whatever she and Jerry found for what was rightfully hers. So Mimi and Jerry drove her brother's borrowed van to the trailer park they had all shared, and while Mimi waited, Jerry crept to Alga's trailer, careful not to step on dry foliage that would give him away. He pulled phone lines out of the terminal on the mobile home, just to make sure Alga couldn't call the cops. It was after midnight, and no sounds or light emerged. Jerry breathed a sigh of relief, not sure how he would have confronted a shouting angry husband. He wasn't good at planning for surprises.

He crept to the pickup truck-camper a few spaces away and rapped. Almost certainly Alga never stayed overnight there, but Jerry wanted to make sure before he drove it off. Followed by Mimi in the van, he drove the camper back to their place in Berkeley, and unloaded its contents into the storage shed. Mimi noticed Alga's old holstered revolver—the gun he had threatened her with—among the contents, but paid little attention to it. They mostly just piled all the stuff in. She asked Jerry to inspect it all later for anything they could barter in exchange for some of her nicer clothes, her hope chest, or a few small antiques she had collected over the years. She thought Alga's electronic gear, some of which was valuable, would turn up. Alga could repair anything with wires, and tinkered with cameras, CB radios, television sets, tape players and the like.

As he handled one item after another, Jerry sighed. The Ford had to be worth a couple thousand, being only four years old, but this stuff would barely raise fifty bucks. Hardly worth the trouble, especially if Alga went to the cops or a lawyer. Since the truck was registered in both names, Alga wasn't likely to press charges, as ex-lawyer Jerry knew.

Jerry turned to leave when he saw an old leather holster with the revolver half-hanging out. It looked huge, and when he pulled it out, he noticed the imprint on the barrel: ".38 Long Colt."

It's in pretty good shape, he thought, certainly in working condition. Alga probably saved it for camping trips. Bears and cougars roamed the California Mountains, and shooting this gun would more than scare them away. It surely would kill any human intruders, Jerry thought. He hefted it again, suddenly noticing that Alga had left it loaded.

That startled him. Loaded weapons meant trouble. His father had let his four sons handle and shoot shotguns, but never handguns or rifles. Even a .22 rifle slug could carry a mile, his dad reminded him many times, and might wound someone's livestock, shatter a window, even kill a neighbor. Though Jerry had grown up with shotguns, he had little experience with handguns. He opened the cylinder cover and shook out four bullets.

The .38 cartridges were thick and corroded, rather ugly really, and ancient. Probably had nestled in that old revolver for years. Jerry squeezed the four cartridges in his hand and decided to throw them away. Would he ever need a handgun? Certainly not a loaded one. He slipped the cartridges into his pants pocket and later pitched them into the dumpster near their apartment, thinking they'd probably never fire anyway.

He gripped the revolver tightly. Mimi had noticed it when they first took the camper, probably because it conjured bad memories of their break-up, when Alga waved it in her face. Jerry kept turning the big gun over in his hand. This was no target or plinking toy like the .22 rifles he had fired as a boy.

He slid the empty weapon back in its holster and wrapped it in a Safeway sack so it looked innocuous. Good thing the barrel was imprinted with the right size ammo, otherwise it probably wouldn't shoot, he thought. Out of all that junk, here was one item that might have value. He decided to just put it away, out of reach of his daughters or Mimi, and see what he could get for it. It probably would come in handy someday—for cash, if nothing else.

2: Family Visit

IN EARLY SPRING of 1975 Wayne Mark called his son Jerry and asked him to fly to Iowa with his two granddaughters. Jerry and his first wife Rebecca were divorcing, so she wasn't invited, nor was Mimi, Jerry's new girlfriend. His father's tumor had grown worse. The cobalt treatments were taking a toll, and Wayne wanted to see Jerry and his granddaughters before he felt too much pain to enjoy their company. Jerry asked Mimi to join him, anxious for her to meet the folks. Mimi reluctantly agreed. Though they couldn't afford it, they scraped together the money for a ticket for Mimi so she could meet the family. She needed to fly back early, but Jerry planned to stay on.

Nothing went right. The old patriarch and Jerry's brothers kept their distance. Though they behaved politely, the Mark men didn't approve of Jerry's hippie California lifestyle—his traveling and living with Mimi before either was even divorced. The Marks were stolid Midwesterners, with core conservative values, which disallowed the looser life that Jerry had adopted, along with his shaggy look and peacenik attitudes. For all they knew, he was a pothead too.

Only Jerry's mother Dorothy seemed to like Mimi. For Dorothy, Jerry could do no wrong. Her soft spot for her second eldest son sometimes set her against Wayne, and a rumor later circulated that the elder Mark wanted to divorce Dorothy at the very end of his life. Bill Sindlinger, the family lawyer, supposedly talked him out of it by detailing catastrophic financial consequences for all of them. The elder Mark was nothing if not pragmatic.

From the first day, Jerry felt like an outsider. The brothers bickered about everything, from estate planning to farming to Wayne's will to Les's emerging position as the Mark family's CEO. That was the worst. Jerry and Les never came to blows, but they shouted over their disagreements, and no one could calm them down. Jerry's temper made him unpredictable. The Marks had warned Rebecca before their marriage about Jerry's volatile temper.

One evening Wayne told Jerry that he and Dorothy were turning their old farmhouse on Union Road, the "homeplace," over to Les and Jorjean. Jerry's face went fiery, and he felt his skin prickle.

Jerry believed that his father's business dealings were morally, maybe even legally wrong. To him, the old man's real estate dealings were unsupportable, and Les would end up screwing Jerry out of his share of the farm, as he had told Alga that spring. This visit only confirmed his worst fears.

On top of that, Jerry's third brother, Tom, was becoming more of a problem. He occasionally drove around Black Hawk County in an old Chevy the family provided, and when he ran out of gas, he abandoned it, and could never remember where. Les had grown weary of hiring tow trucks to haul the Chevy back to his place, so he took away Tom's keys. Jerry felt more pity than affection for Tom, and felt they all needed to put more money away from their inheritance to pay for serious hospitalization and possibly a cure for Tom's mental problems. This would cost a bundle, and neither Les nor Wayne thought Tom was curable. They shouted about that too, with no resolution.

Richard, the eldest brother, made piety his profession and didn't communicate much with the family, least of all Jerry. In fact, he had created a new life for himself in the ministry in Toronto, and paid little attention to his Iowa family's problems. In many ways, there were two Mark families: Dorothy and Jerry formed one unit, and Wayne and Les the other, with Richard and Tom more or less disconnected from either.

The homeplace had been in the Mark family for decades, and they owned all the land around it, plus more around the county. By the mid-1970s the farms that Les and his father worked came to over 1200 acres of some of the richest topsoil in the world. And both Wayne and Les were intent on acquiring more prime ag land, adding smaller farms whenever possible to their holdings.

The Marks' considerable wealth intimidated many farmers and neighbors, and their aloof ways didn't sit well with modest rural Midwesterners. Jerry saw Les following in his father's footsteps, but felt powerless to stop him. Jerry felt he deserved better. Now his younger brother stood to get it all. One night around the dinner table in early June, Jerry, Les, and Wayne finally had it out. It had been building for days. Dorothy and Jorjean stayed in the kitchen, trying not to listen, but hearing every word. By then Mimi had flown back to Berkeley.

Wayne, feeling shaky but still able to speak his mind, asked Jerry straight out, "So what's with farming these days? Do you want to come back and work the land?"

Before Jerry could answer, Les piped up. "I want to say, Dad, that we've asked Jerry about this before, but it's all talk. I don't mean to act like you're not here, Jerry, but really you haven't been. You pitch in for a day or two, then go off with your buddies, talking politics, taking some road trip. We wanted to count on you, but couldn't. I've even had some delivery guys tell me that if you come back, they won't work with us anymore. So I'd just as soon not have you back." He looked at his older sibling straight on, unflinching and unsmiling.

This brutal candor caught Jerry off guard. Les was still a boy, really, so telling his older brother he couldn't return to farm their own land came as a jolt. Farming was the one thing they had done together over the years.

Their dad jumped into the silence. "Well, Jerry, Les told you what he thinks. What do you think?"

His face growing hot and his jaw clenching, Jerry boiled. "You two have your minds made up. You've probably worked this all out so you could break the news to me slowly. I can't fight both of you."

Les and Wayne both jumped in, talking at once, "No, no, we haven't even brought it up…," they began.

Jerry stopped them, "Now, goddammit, shut up and listen. You know, Dad, that you've set us against each other. Remember when you told me that Les didn't know how to plant a straight cornrow? And I tried to show him, and he got pissed? You can't tell me you didn't know that would hack him off, and we didn't speak for two days."

The old man came back at him. "Jerry, you had better not blame me for your rotten work habits. You're not a worker. You'd rather sit around with your hippie friends than get anything done. What have you done since you left? Nothing. You know that's true."

That cut Jerry deep. He shouted straight at his father. "Goddammit, you don't know shit! For Christ's sake, Dad, I was working like hell here summers during high school and after I graduated when Les was chasing junior high girls. I taught him how to farm better than you ever did. You need to figure out who's the real farmer in this family!" His face stayed crimson.

Both Les and Wayne looked at Jerry like he had just round-housed them. Les spoke first. "Jerry, you have no right to talk to Dad like that. You know he's given us plenty, including a good chunk of inheritance money, and now you sit here spitting on it. You should be ashamed."

Their father stayed silent, looking at the floor and searching for words.

Then Jerry slashed and burned. "You think I'm spitting on it? Well get this," and he turned to stare at his father directly, "Old man, when you die, I'll come back to piss on your grave." He had said it quietly while directing it straight at them. His words struck home like bullets.

Neither Les nor Wayne could speak. They stared at the floor in silence. Jerry knew enough to get out, then and there. Striding out the door, he gathered up his daughters and shooed them to bed. He had planned to stay another week, but this visit was over. He'd get his daughters down to see Rebecca's parents, then head up to Nebraska to see his friend Renato. That was his plan. There was no closing this gaping wound in the Mark family.

Meanwhile, Les and Wayne stayed silent. Finally Les shook his head and tried to soothe his father. "Dad, you didn't deserve that. You know Jerry's a hothead. He's jealous, and just damned lazy."

His father nodded wearily and called for Dorothy and Jorjean to join them in the den. No one spoke. Jorjean rubbed Les's shoulders to comfort him. They shook their heads, murmuring regrets, and soon went to bed. Jerry and his daughters left the next morning with a few cool goodbyes.

By mid-June, life had gotten back to normal on the Mark farm, with plans running full-on for Les and Jorjean to move into the homeplace in September, the elder Marks to move into a smaller house up the road, and Les to take over the Mark farms and real estate business as CEO.

3: Planning

JERRY MARK FLEW home to Berkeley consumed with fury. His mind churned with hurt and rage, making him almost physically ill as he squirmed in his seat on the big jet. Nothing made sense, least of all his family. Both daughters thought he seemed weird, and his ill temper, combined with his dark mood, scared them. They avoided him.

He sulked and fumed, then worried. God, to have insulted and cursed a dying father. My damned temper again, he thought. Still, he grinned as he remembered how the old man glared at him as he received that "piss on your grave" insult. If looks could kill. Karmic revenge for all the pain he caused, maybe. Shifting his position, he winced from an old tailbone injury his father had inflicted years before. Kicked him, hard, during some fight or another.

Then he felt shame. His own dad, the man who had willed him good money, most of which he had already borrowed and spent against his inheritance. What the hell was he thinking? Would the old man cut him off? He groaned. Doing wrong never bothered him so much as getting caught.

Then there was Les. Jerry broke into a cold sweat when he thought about his little brother moving into the homeplace and running the real estate operation. Les had taken Jerry into his confidence one night shortly after he arrived and bragged, or so Jerry thought, about how much more the Mark real estate operation was pulling in since he had started managing it. So too with their farms. All turning a tidy profit.

Les had surprised his older brother with his success. Jerry could hardly believe how well Les managed the business side. How in hell did the kid brother learn balance sheets and financial shenanigans so fast? He was still just a boy, dammit. Remorseless moneygrubber, just like the old man. Those two really did know how to bring in the dough. But money wasn't the answer. Always the idealist, Jerry sought justice, truth, and peace. Not money.

The elder Mark wasn't much liked or trusted, but young Les, with his winning smile and lively wife and kids, could do no wrong for folks who came to him for advice on farm real estate. Les would no doubt screw them too, just like the old man. The sins of the fathers. He shifted again from pain, which always hurt worse when he flew.

Les was fast becoming the family CEO. Goddammit anyway. Jerry pounded the armrest as the 707 winged over Nebraska. He felt crushed, and knew that come September when Les and Jorjean moved, it was going to grate him to the bone. His idealism made him flinch at the likelihood that Les and the old man were greedy and probably unethical. Goddamned capitalists. Political rallies around Berkeley attracted him, where capitalists were arch-villains. That made sense to him. His own family, money-mad and greedy.

The 707's four engines created just enough steady thrumming to make drifting off seem automatic, especially given his bone-deep fatigue. He had found little enjoyment during his visit with Renato, his old Brazilian Peace Corps friend who had moved to Nebraska. Much of their time together Jerry had complained about Les and his father. Renato told him to forget it and get on with his new life with Mimi, but Jerry seemed inconsolable, even obsessed.

As the 707 jet winged over Colorado, dreams and visions arose, some from better times. Remembering his senior year in high school when little Les was entering fifth grade, he felt a pang of nostalgia. Their seven-year age difference kept them from becoming brother-buddies, but they did develop a mentor-pupil relationship, and Les certainly admired his older brother's popularity and good reputation around town.

Still, Jerry sometimes felt a vague, odd, uneasiness around Les. It was the same stress he felt around his father. To Jerry, Les seemed to know more than he expressed, and therefore seemed to feel quietly superior, always in control. He felt no such control, often going red and blustering. So he envied Les for his quiet confidence, but hated Les's superior, confident demeanor. The arrogant twerp, he thought.

Les sometimes had come to him for advice about school, especially playground bullies. Though Jerry was no hulking bruiser, he certainly could threaten fifth-grade bullies that occasionally descended on Les. Most of the time, Jerry told Les to fight his own battles. "I'm not your bodyguard," he groused.

The only bad fight during those years came back to him, vividly. He pondered it from his perspective as the outsider brother. One of Jerry's friends loaned him a dozen old Playboys that the friend had spirited away from his dad's collection, and Jerry kept the soft-core treasures hidden in an old chest beneath some sweaters in his room. One afternoon Jerry went to find them, and damned if they weren't missing. It had to be Les. Tom wasn't at all interested, and in fact never messed with Jerry's stuff, and Richard was long gone, but Jerry had often caught Les rummaging in his room.

His temper flared, and he vowed that he'd grab his sneak-thief brother and teach him a good lesson. First he wanted to find his borrowed contraband, since his friend wanted them back, then he'd give Les a good whack or two. Jerry stalked into Les's room and searched everywhere he could, but found nothing. The little jerk knew how to hide stuff, he gave him that.

A few minutes later Dorothy and Wayne drove in with Les. Jerry ran downstairs and confronted his little brother. In a hard whisper, while the folks were still outside, he spit out "You little shit, where the hell are my magazines? What did you do with them? You stay out of my room, goddammit!" He whacked his little brother, hard, on the shoulder. Too hard. Les began to cry, then scream. Dorothy heard and came in.

"What's going on? Les? What's the matter?"

"Jerry broke my shoulder," he wailed, and ran to her, cradling his injury. Dorothy hollered back at Jerry.

"JERRY! Don't bully your brother! You know better. You're bigger and you're supposed to protect him, not beat him up. By the way, your dad found those dirty magazines you've been hiding. He heard about them from Charles at Rotary, and knew you hid them somewhere. He took them away yesterday."

At that news, Les's sore shoulder seemed to have healed, and he began snickering. "I didn't do it, you stinkwad," he yelled at Jerry.

Jerry grimaced from the memory. He still blamed Les for the fact that he *might* have stolen them, which meant he still deserved a good whack. But most of all Jerry blamed the old man for not respecting his right to privacy, for not even asking him about them before taking them away. Goddamn girlie mags, he could hear his father mutter. One more reason he never liked me much. The old bastard had never been young, thought Jerry ruefully.

Then he dozed, falling into a dream. It wasn't quite a lucid dream, that kind of dream where you seem awake and aware, but it still left a powerful impression. He would have similar vivid dreams later, but he remembered this one for years, and never understood it.

It began as so many of his dreams did, with walking down cornrows while detasseling. He was sweating, dripping from moisture-laden air and a blazing sun. A typical detasseler's day. Then a cool wind whipped, the sky darkened, and he felt blessed relief. A heavy mist seemed to hover over the field. The longer he trudged, the blacker the field became until he could barely see the earth at his feet.

Just as he began to feel lost and frightened, a translucent azure wall shimmered ahead. It provided a ghostly light in the dark field, and he moved quickly toward it. As he drew closer, he saw that the wall wasn't a wall at all, but a mass of heavy gelatinous matter, neither solid nor liquid. As he neared the wall, it radiated coolness, like a mountain of icy gel.

Without hesitation Jerry waded into it. It refreshed him, and he sighed long and hard. Offering support, it made him drift and float as if on a cloud. As he moved through it, he heard thunder booming above him, and for a few moments feared a lightning strike. His fear gave way to elation as he wafted through the cool mass. At last, he thought. I'm moving toward something, something important.

Then the gelatinous material began to solidify. It transformed into heavy slush, then ice, as though the temperature were steadily dropping. Finally he felt frozen in the mass of ice up to his neck. It was the strangest sensation, and he should have felt terror, a sense of his own annihilation. Instead he only felt at peace, a calm that told him he could move ahead without fear of losing control.

The suffocating heat of the Iowa cornfield had given way to cold immobility. Jerry felt nothing but relief, the weight of his family gone, his entire being stabilized by ice. Though surrounded by darkness, he felt safe, protected by ice, which acted like a suit of armor.

Then the jet bumped from turbulence, and he stirred into wakefulness. The stewardess asked if he wanted a snack, and he nodded, realizing that he felt relaxed for the first time in days. Elated, even.

What a wonderful dream, he thought. What the hell did it mean? He smiled at having felt such deep relief from the summer heat and humidity he had endured so many years. The cold beckoned to him, engulfed him, relieved him.

Mimi met Jerry and his daughters at the gate. He felt glad to see her, but kept his distance. After her welcome home hug, she shivered. She couldn't remember him feeling so physically cold, almost like he was taking ill from some nasty virus.

Jerry spent the next few days dawdling at part-time work, brooding, wondering what to do next. He had no plan, though plenty of motivation. Barking and growling at Mimi about everything, he could feel her withdrawing. To Mimi he seemed cold and cocooned, unable to live with anyone, including himself.

Finally a plan surfaced. He remembered that untraceable revolver. Why not fix this problem once and for all? The vision of how he could do it formed, at first hazily, then into focus. A motorcycle could be outfitted for long-haul riding. He could jump on I-80 and get to Iowa in probably three days. Not easy, but doable and back in two, hitching a ride, maybe.

His legal training made him both cautious and optimistic. He knew he was smart, far smarter than the low-level detectives they would put on the case from Black Hawk County, and at least as smart as the State BCI guys. He could tell Mimi he needed to find himself, and buy a big enough bike with another loan from his father. He needed to find the right ammo. And he would cut his hair and beard so he wouldn't draw attention. His brilliant idea: call Mimi from the road, telling her where he stayed overnight, and she would end up providing am airtight alibi. All of a sudden he could see it happening.

He began making mental checklists of needed gear—a cold weather riding suit, a wind faring and luggage box for the bike, camping equipment and food.

Finally it made sense, a plan he could justify for his own long-term good. Fix that family problem permanently, become part of the working world again. Do something at last. With Mimi as his inadvertent partner, he could pull it off.

Soon after, Mimi noticed that he had become easier to live with, more good humored. She encouraged him to take that ride. It couldn't hurt.

Jerry soon asked his father for a loan to buy a car he could use to find work. Wayne Mark obliged with a check for $1,500. On October 3rd

Jerry Mark bought a used Honda 450 motorcycle. It came with a wind faring and rear luggage box.

Seventeen days later, he rode that Honda down to San Luis Obispo to see his estranged wife Rebecca and his daughters, where they helped him cut his hair and shave off his thick beard. On the way home, he stopped at Ken's Sporting Goods Store in Paso Robles. He was looking for .38 Long Colt ammunition.

4: Ammunition

JACK MAKENDONSKY ENJOYED being part owner of Ken's Sporting Goods Store. He got to know people, and being a former Midwesterner, had developed a friendly way with customers that kept them coming back. Ken's sold practically everything for hunters, campers, and fishermen, and carried a large stock of guns and ammo, which comprised a fair part of the store's business. A typical transaction would involve a greeting and helping a customer find what he or she wanted, making small talk based on some common experience, and ringing it up. He seldom remembered customers unless they returned, or unless they did or said something unusual.

On October 20, 1975, a customer he had never seen entered the store, asked for a box of .38 Long Colt cartridges, and showed his driver's license, paying with cash. Makendonski noticed the young man was in his thirties—close to his own age—and he was from Cedar Falls, Iowa. Makendonski himself had been born in Waterloo.

"I see you're from Iowa—I was born in Waterloo, and you're from Cedar Falls.

Small world, eh?"

"Yeah," said the customer. "What brought you to California?"

"Weather and work, like everyone else. Hated those long Iowa winters, and there wasn't much to do around there except work at Deere's or Rath Packing. I wanted some sun and more choices."

"I don't blame you. I like it out here too, and won't go back." He picked up the box of cartridges.

Later Makendonski couldn't remember the customer's features well enough to identify him, either from a photograph or in a lineup. He did remember the guy was polite.

5: Ride to Iowa

TUESDAY AFTERNOON, October 28th, Jerry Mark finished packing and gassed up the Honda, knowing he needed to hit the road Wednesday morning. He needed to make six to seven hundred miles daily, more if possible.

He wrote and mailed Les a letter the day before with the following paragraph:

> "If you could write a letter of recommendation that details my work habits, this would enable me to present a much more stable and responsible employment history than I am otherwise able to do, and that would be most helpful in the job market. I believe I am generally informed enough about your operation to respond to questions concerning such hypothetical employment in an adequate manner during job interviews, so it would be a low-risk falsehood in the circumstances. You could respond to any inquiries made by

my prospective employers based upon your actual operation, modifying it only to the extent to pretend that we were general operating partners. If this is agreeable to you I would appreciate it greatly…"

He didn't know when it would arrive at Les's but it would show that he and his brother were still close.

That night he didn't sleep well, and kicked himself later when fatigue set in. He kept waking to Mimi's light snoring, and felt unusually annoyed with her. He tapped her shoulder a few times, but she only murmured and kept snoring. They had no other sleeping room, so he dozed, awoke, dreamed and dozed off, tossing and turning through the night.

He saw himself in dream-fragments, dumping the Honda on a slick road and spending days in the hospital. Then he somehow lost the .38 and gave up the whole trip since he wanted nothing to do with trying to find another untraceable gun. Dreaming about utter frustration and defeat, he rode back to Mimi to lie about finding himself. He put a good face on it, but felt completely bereft. A fiasco.

After that he gave up real sleep. When he finally rolled out of bed at six, he felt tired, but counted on adrenaline and No-Doz caffeine pills to keep him going. He avoided street amphetamines, widely available as "white cross," or "black beauties," knowing those drugs' effects were unpredictable. He needed a clear head.

Wednesday morning Mimi got up with him and got ready for work, as usual. She worked as a technician for a chemical company in Berkeley, and had to punch an eight-to-four time clock. It paid the bills.

As she left for work, she gave him a hug. "You ready to ride?" Jerry kissed her goodbye, saying "Yeah, I'm off. I'll see you probably Saturday afternoon. Remember to stick by the phone for the next few nights so we can talk."

"OK, go for it. Come back ready and willing." She was out the door, and Jerry waved as she drove off. Daytime temperatures hung in the fifties and sixties in California so he wouldn't need long johns or the winter riding suit until he hit mountains in Utah and Wyoming. He ate a bowl of Cheerios while glancing again at the map, tracing his route up I-80 toward Salt Lake City. Grabbing a bag of trail mix and a sandwich, he placed the bags with other gear into his backpack.

He calmly strode to their storage shed, made sure no one was looking, broke the cheap lock by smacking it hard with a hammer from their household toolbox, and rummaged around inside to make it look burglarized. He left the broken lock hanging and removed his Iowa license plate. He had already stowed the revolver in the Honda's luggage box.

Around 9:00 he climbed on the Honda and pushed the starter button. It sputtered, rumbled to life. Always dependable starters, those Hondas. Pulling his helmet down, he felt the bike's 450cc motor's steady vibrations move up his spine. It was a quiet bike, almost shockingly so compared to a Harley, small or large. Still, he faced one hell of a long ride. And there would be plenty of vibration as the hours passed, the Honda being a two-banger. Long-distance bikers preferred four-cylinder engines due to less vibration and a smoother road feel. But they were considerably more expensive, and this Honda fit his meager budget. He knew his back was going to pain him mightily—but no pain, no gain.

At first he rode slowly, barely the speed limit until he hit the on-ramp for I-580 up to Interstate 80. Then he kicked it. Anticipating the defining event of his life, he entered a strange physical high, the first of many adrenalin surges that would keep him focused and energized. He knew he was doing the right thing, that he was about to change his life for the better. If he succeeded—and how could he fail? —he'd probably never have to work again, or at least work as hard as he did as a Legal

Aid lawyer, which drove him crazy. Best of all, he could finally exorcise his all-consuming rage. Chills ran up his spine, calmed him. At times he wondered if his actual body temperature had gone down since his trip to Iowa.

He rolled past a set of Interstate Signs: North to I-80, South to I-880—and knew as he pointed the Honda north he would have to start lying, or at least making excuses. Now if anyone saw him, and there were plenty of rest stops where they would, he might have to admit that he took the north exit on a whim, and traveled hundreds of miles into Nevada. He wished he were invisible, slicing silently through space like an arrow. No such luck; he knew people would notice and remember him, but tried not to worry. Short hair and a clean-shaven look would help.

He opened the throttle, and the Honda quickly hit 80 mph. Too fast. He slowed, settled into the left half of the right lane, and relaxed for the long haul, knowing he would vibrate ten hours a day on that hard vinyl saddle, more with breaks. He hoped for a downright boring ride, with no surprises, no breakdowns, no side trips or distractions, and definitely no speeding tickets. He only had to hang on, gas up, stay awake, and try not to attract attention.

Before long he was lulled into an altered state of consciousness, though alert to hazards and speed, and the miles began to rack up. He pegged the speedometer at just over sixty and kept it there, watching the gas gauge. Though he knew that the new gas-saving speed limit—enacted in 1974 because of the Arab oil embargo—was 55, or "double nickels" he also knew that highway cops seldom bothered with any-one doing sixty or slightly above. Between 60 and 65, he could make around 500 miles in an eight-hour day. If he could manage 12 hours on the road with breaks, he could make 650-700 miles in two days, and around 400-500 miles on Friday. That was his plan.

Knowing he needed gas around every two hours, he planned a fill-up routine. He'd pull into the busiest truck stop he could find, roll to the self-service pumps, keep the visor down, pay cash inside and leave. No chatting, no snacks, only a bathroom break if the men's room wasn't occupied. He drank as little as possible, stopping at pull-offs that looked deserted and urinating in the weeds. Though this slowed him down, he avoided opportunities for identification. He never looked directly at clerks, nor they at him, he hoped.

With a full tank, which would carry him anywhere from 125 to 140 miles, he hit cruising speed fast and sank into a familiar riding lull. Two chores he needed to complete sometime before Iowa, probably well into Nebraska—disconnecting the Honda's odometer, and exchanging his Iowa plate for the California tag. Get to eastern Nebraska, he thought, find a deserted pullout and get them done fast.

Past Sacramento he passed a sign for "Iowa Hill," an old gold rush town off I-80 supposedly named in the 1850s by the Iowa miners who discovered it. For years it enjoyed a boom, sitting upon gold mine claims that yielded millions by the 1880s. Now it was a sleepy little city where tourists inspected mined-out old gold diggings. Brochures and guides told stories of those gold rush days, from boom to bust, beginning with Iowa gold miners who struck it big. Jerry couldn't help but feel a tug of temptation to visit the place, and probably would have had he been riding for fun.

In spite of his anger toward his family, he felt affection for his home state. It always comforted him to know that Iowa stood as a beacon of normalcy in a crazy country. He hummed past Reno and pushed on toward Utah as fast as he dared. Fatigue so far hadn't been an issue, thanks to healthy amounts of adrenalin pumping through his system. His plan still made sense, with no worries other than trying to remain unnoticed. Such were his thoughts as he rode along I-80 into north-eastern Nevada on Wednesday afternoon. His determination drove him on as much as the Honda's dependable motor, humming its four-cycle two-cylinder song.

Well past Reno and still 300 miles from Utah, Jerry began to feel the first signs of fatigue—buzzing lower body, aching in that chronic troublesome tailbone, dangerous temptations to nod off. It was late afternoon—he hadn't made especially good time—and his snack bar lunch didn't fill him up, so he felt downright sleepy. His arms and legs seemed close to cramping up. Badly needing a break, he knew that if he pushed himself too far he could lose control. Everything happens fast on a speeding motorcycle. So he rode until he needed both gas and food for a third fill. Pulling into a 7-Eleven, he bought a hot bratwurst from a rolling electric grill, a couple of fruit pies and an apple. As he paid, the clerk asked, "How you like that Honda? I've been thinking about gettin' a 450. Does it ride as good as it looks?"

Alarmed at being noticed, Jerry engaged the young guy as little as possible. "Yeah, it's fine. Sorry, I've gotta keep going" and strode out the door. He figured the guy barely saw him. Wearily, he climbed back on the Honda and found a side road down from the 7-Eleven, pulled off near what appeared to be a shade tree, hauled out his riding suit, spread it out, sat down to eat, and lay down.

He seemed to drift, almost float, for a few minutes, his arms and legs burning and buzzing, his tailbone throbbing, but not as much as he feared. He had never ridden so far for so long, and worried that he might not have the stamina or physical strength. Then he fell asleep, heavy enough to dream. Images came: floating eyes, set in distorted half-animal, half-human faces. His dream-self took refuge in a closet in his apartment, then the basement of the homeplace, then a steel locker in his old high school, but eyes still watched and saw him. Stirring, he felt a surge of panic as he bolted awake, sweating. Taking several deep breaths, he stared at the vast Nevada landscape lying bright before him in the afternoon sun. "Only a dream," he murmured, and shook it off.

If he believed in omens, he might have turned around. Jerry believed in logic and reason, and didn't bother with supernatural speculating. Certainly not benevolent forces who kept watch.

He stood up slowly, feeling older than his 33 years, stretched long and hard, rolled his head to stretch his neck, and remembered to call Mimi. Just past Lovelock, he thought—around 300 miles from Berkeley. Rolling back to the 7-Eleven, he found a pay phone and punched "o" on the keypad. "Collect call to Berkeley, California. Merrilyn Forrest at this number—" The phone rang only twice, and Mimi answered, accepting charges.

"Hi Mimi. I'm on the open road, havin' a great time. Wish I could say I wish you were here, but you'd hate it."

"Hi. Good to hear you're alive. How far did you get?"

"Not all that far. Got down to Coalinga, close to the Mojave Desert. Not a city here, just a bend in the road. Beautiful country."

"So why would anybody hate it? Sounds nice, and we could be together."

"You'd like it fine in a car, but not on the back of a Honda. I'm about done in. I'm going to crash and get back to you tomorrow night, OK?"

"OK, Jerry. I already miss you. Stay safe, get your head right. Love you."

"Bye Mimi. Love you too."

He hung up, pleased that she didn't ask more questions, and hoped she'd remember Coalinga as his first night's stop. Riding hard, he needed to make Cheyenne by late Thursday—over 800 miles from Lovelock. As he neared Elko, Nevada, serious fatigue stalked him, made him slow down. This alarmed him, since he had barely ridden 500 miles.

Jerry Mark was no long-haul biker. Had he underestimated how much energy and concentration keeping a bike going for ten hours would take? He needed more than a nap. Past Elko, he pulled off to find a secluded patch of bare ground for camping. Now he felt OK about how the trip was evolving. He would need all day Thursday, but he could make Cheyenne. From Cheyenne across Nebraska into Iowa would make a long day Friday, but he could do it. Then sleep came, and he was gone to the world.

Well before dawn, Jerry awoke to a cacophony of twittering birds. Nature's alarm clocks, he thought, and loved that idea. On his own, wild and free, like Hopper and Fonda in *Easy Rider*. He packed up, heading back toward I-80 to Cheyenne. He rode a hundred more miles before needing breakfast, got off at Wendover, on the Nevada-Utah border. Feeling energized and rested, his mission kept him focused and clear, adrenaline doing its work.

By 9:00 he was riding the nearly uninhabited stretch between Wendover and Salt Lake City. It was only 120 miles, barely two hours at his speed, but it seemed to take twice that. No towns, almost no traffic except for omnipresent semis hauling the nation's cargo east. About as dull a ride as it gets, and it was getting cold.

The Newfoundland Mountain Range to the north broke the horizon, but nothing to the south. East of Wendover he saw signs for the Bonneville Salt Flats, and knew he was riding an ancient lakebed, flat as a skillet. Land speed records had been set and broken there for decades. Bonneville had become one of Utah's major tourist attractions, at least when someone was trying to make land-speed history. If he were on his vision quest he would have stopped for a look, but Jerry Mark was no tourist.

As the miles racked up, the steady pull of the Honda's 450ccs lulled him into daydreams. Passing a skinny young female hitchhiker, he wondered about picking her up. Man, that could be fun. It would take his mind off everything. Of course he had no time, but imagined she would be lonely, talkative, and OK with sex. A hippie chick hitching east from Haight-Ashbury. He'd call her "Ginger," a nice hippie chick name. Probably traveling with a stash of weed. Grinning at the fantasy, he gave his mind a break from the tedium of the ride.

They would roll around a few hours, balling, as hippies called it, and he would get back on the road a happy man. If worse came to worse and the cops discovered he had lied about his stops, he would tell them that he picked up "Ginger" and didn't want to tell Mimi his real location, since she would start asking questions. He was forming a powerful connection with her, and screwing some hitchhiker wasn't conducive to long-term romance. As Salt Lake City appeared on the eastern far horizon like a mirage, shimmering in a pall of light gray, he finally shook off the daydream and re-focused.

It wasn't yet noon and he was two-thirds of the way across Utah. As he moved relatively slowly through Salt Lake City on state highways (I-80 wouldn't be completed west of Salt Lake City for 11 more years) he saw signs for Provo, a few miles south of Salt Lake City. Tonight he would phone Mimi about camping near Provo. That would be about the right distance from Coalinga for a long day's ride. He was headed for Cheyenne, though, hundreds of miles east. Once he got past Salt Lake City, it was I-80 all the way, less than 450 miles to Cheyenne. His second day was proving much longer than the first. Hard, but he could handle it. By the time he hit Cheyenne, he would have traveled over 1100 miles on the Honda in two days.

That Thursday afternoon passed quickly. Mile after mile of I-80 rolled under him from Salt Lake City to Cheyenne. Western names from his map slid by on green Interstate signs: Green River, Reliance, Bitter Creek, Table Rock, Rawlins, Walcott, the Medicine Bow National Forest. He maintained an almost dreamy state of consciousness, re-laxed but alert, watching his speed and the gas gauge. Making good time, he slowed down for Laramie by dinnertime and stayed there for another burger and fries. An occasional No-Doz helped. They boosted his alertness, and were available everywhere. Each pill offered the same jolt as two strong cups of coffee.

At that point he sat only 50 miles from Cheyenne, over 800 miles from his first stop in Lovelock the day before. He had been on the road for 14 hours and felt ragged. Another hour to Cheyenne and that was it. As he rolled past the city limits, he pulled into another 7-Eleven—they were everywhere, it seemed—and though it was early for their 9:00 phone date, called Mimi, again collect.

"Hi Jerry. Still finding yourself?" She sounded cheerful.

"Yep, been riding all day, still having a great time. That Honda's a super road bike. Hasn't missed a beat. I made it into Utah, somewhere near Provo, and I'm settling in."

"Utah? I'm impressed. I didn't know you were going that far. That's a ways out there, isn't it?"

"Yeah, a good long ride from Coalinga. But I didn't sleep that much last night, and I love this bike. It's so much fun that I felt like going a ways. Feels like I'm on an adventure. I've stopped a few places to look around. I could make a career out of this."

"Yeah, I figured. Jerry, don't you dare start to like biking too much. Get yourself found and come home. I miss you. Where are you again?"

"Provo, Utah."

After their "I love yous" he hung up and looked at his map. According to his calculations, Cheyenne sat 760 miles west of the homeplace. That would take another fourteen hours with breaks and fills. Then he had to find energy for his family errand. Tomorrow was probably going to be the longest and hardest day of his life, he thought. He had to get some serious sleep and roll out at the crack of dawn. He reminded himself that he didn't have to arrive anywhere near the homeplace until after midnight Friday.

That night he slept hard and long. It was cold, but he didn't feel it—only the satisfaction that his plan seemed on schedule. As he stirred awake at his makeshift campsite outside Cheyenne he couldn't remember any dreams, nor did he harbor any last minute doubts. He packed up quickly and rode onto I-80 by 6:00 AM, gliding like a missile toward Iowa.

He had last filled the tank outside Cheyenne, so he could ride well into Nebraska without stopping. As he crossed the Wyoming-Nebraska border he felt he was crossing a larger and scarier boundary. In a way, though he was entering completely familiar territory, he was crossing an uncharted point of no return. He could justify riding to Wyoming, even well into it, even as far as Cheyenne. But he couldn't justify getting into Nebraska unless he stopped there and turned around. If he kept going, questions would arise that he couldn't answer. His mother would ask why he rode that far and didn't come to Iowa. And his friend Renato in Norfolk would wonder the same, expecting his old buddy to ride up from I-80 for a visit. If some investigator put him in the Midwest, even western Nebraska, they would begin looking for eyewitnesses who spotted him in Iowa. His natural sense of self-preservation and survival began to kick in, and the adrenalin flowed. Adrenalin, in fact, would keep him going for the next 36 hours.

He pulled into a gas station/restaurant west of Chappell, Nebraska, 120 miles out of Cheyenne, around 8:30 in the morning for another fill. He realized that he hadn't had any breakfast, so he found a booth and ordered coffee, juice, three scrambled eggs, bacon, hash browns. Standard Midwest farmer fare—greasy, heavy, and filling. It tasted really good, he thought, and noticed how hungry he kept getting. This long-distance riding took plenty of energy, and he didn't want to stop for big meals. When he did, he ate large. He bought three breakfast rolls and wrapped them for later, along with a quart of milk. That would keep him going. He felt a raw chill in the air and realized that even with the sun full out, the temperature hovered around fifty. He pulled out his cold weather riding suit and stepped into it, feeling immediately cozy. Barring a big temperature drop, he wouldn't be shivering all that much. He later lined newspapers under the suit since the temperature in Iowa dropped to just above freezing, and with the highway wind, he might get too cold to ride. But cold still didn't bother him as much as heat.

Chappell was a tiny town. Though a county seat, population was so sparse in this part of Nebraska that barely a thousand people called it home. Even in Iowa, most county seat towns were more populated than that. This would be a good place to call it quits and turn around, he mused. Far enough to justify a good long bike ride but not so far that it's close to Iowa.

Vowing to remember Chappell as his turn-around town, he rode back to I-80 bound for Iowa. Nebraska, charting west to east on I-80, is wider than Iowa by some 150 miles, so it was a 450-mile drive straight across the Cornhusker State.

He knew it would take him into the evening hours to get to Iowa and at least another four to get to Northeast Iowa, taking I-80 past Des Moines, then over to one of the two-lane highways north, straight to Ackley, then Finchford. He would take a different route home, down I-35 to I-80, just to avoid hitting the same rest stops twice. Two-lane roads meant more traffic, easier to get a ticket, easier to be noticed, and more highway patrol. That worried him. A 1900-mile trip to Iowa from Berkeley in three days for fun made no sense. Especially with winter bearing down, it was too damned much work, especially for a guy who had never ridden Interstates on a bike.

The closer Iowa loomed, the more determined he felt. Having spent all this effort not just on the ride, but on the time, planning, his dad's loan, the lies, the bad dreams, the psychic energy, the feeling of moving into a very dark side of his personality—he couldn't stop now. Too much invested to slink back home with nothing but bitterness inside. He felt his anger toward Les and his father welling up, calling forth a familiar cool rage. It never diminished.

Around 9:30 that morning he pulled into the rest area east of Chappell and cleaned up. The attendant noticed him, but they talked only briefly, Jerry making sure it was all right to use the sinks to clean up. He washed his face, used the toilet, and left, sure that the Nebraska attendant wouldn't remember him. He had parked the Honda well away so it couldn't easily be seen from the building.

He rode on another 100 miles, then decided to pull off and bolt on the Iowa license plates and disconnect the odometer. He took a nondescript off-ramp and rode a couple of miles north to a small pull-off into a cornfield. He turned the Honda off and looked around. Except for the distant whine of I-80, only a light wind whispered. No traffic for miles either way, it seemed. If anyone was coming or going, he thought, he would wave, pull out his blanket and sit down with his lunch.

Since no cars appeared from either direction, he opened the luggage box, pulled out the Iowa plate, removed the California tag and bolted on the Iowa plate. He would need to remember to replace the California plate somewhere in Wyoming coming back.

He stood up and loosened the threaded cap that held the odometer cable in place. He let the cable stand up loose against the gas tank, and though that might look suspicious, there was no way he could leave the cable loose but still hooked into the speedometer, since it would begin registering miles. Ideally he should saw off the end of the cable so he could bolt it back into the speedometer with not enough of the cable left to engage the odometer. But he carried no hacksaw and the half-inch of exposed cable was too strong to break off with the small pliers from the toolkit. So he let the bolt and cable dangle. Besides, with a snapped cable, if anyone inspected the bike closely, they would find the tampering, immediately raising suspicion. This way he would just hook it up later to show the right number of miles for his story. The speedometer registered just over 1600 miles from Berkeley, and he would hook it up later. Just so it didn't show enough to get him clear to Iowa and at least partly back.

That Friday's ride seemed much like Thursday's, with Nebraska town names going by between gas stops, names that Jerry had actually heard from friends who had headed into Nebraska for road trips on I-80. North Platte, Kearny, Grand Island, Lincoln, and finally the heart of the Midwest: Omaha. Home of the Strategic Air Command, Aksar-ben Arena, and the giant meatpackers that butchered and packed corn-fed beef that America and the world loved so much. He had been to Omaha for 4-H activities and always enjoyed the city, but never felt tempted to move there. He was a country boy at heart, and had he gotten along better with his father, might still be farming.

Toward late afternoon, he rolled over the Missouri River Bridge into Council Bluffs, and pulled into the Iowa Welcome Center. "Iowa Welcomes You—Greetings from the Hon. Robert D. Ray, Governor of Iowa," proclaimed a sign near the modest little tourist center. Thoroughly Midwestern. Though he dare not be seen enough to be remembered here, he realized the homeplace sat barely 250 miles away.

After his interminable daily rides, that seemed but a short jump. Yet if he were going to turn tail, this would be the time. He could head back to Omaha, tell Mimi he was staying somewhere in western Nebraska, start home on Saturday, and no one would know what he had planned.

That would mean a return to his increasingly sorry life in Berkeley. A failed lawyer, a Peace Corps volunteer who didn't pursue whatever avenues might have opened, an odd-jobber and adulterer, a divorced husband, a man with a permanent grudge. That was no life when he could be running a large real estate business, a big-time farming business, a bit of philanthropy, some side businesses, maybe a stint as a journalist, even teaching college courses now and then. No worries about money or work or status. His parents would finally be proud of him.

He started the Honda and nosed it back on I-80 east. Now nearly all the small-town names seemed familiar. He had ridden this stretch in high school for trips to Omaha and had gotten used to it. In Iowa, I-80 offered the fastest east-west highway, and it was by far the most traveled road. Jerry buzzed along, headed past I-35 to take backroad two-laners north.

By mid-evening Friday he had gotten just past Des Moines and gassed up at Newton, realizing he was getting close. He didn't want anyone identifying him so near his home, so he took the least traveled roads, turning at Stuart to hit Iowa 117, a two-lane blacktop that might be called the scenic route if central Iowa were actually scenic after late October frosts.

Jerry took his time, stopping in a rest area for a smoke. No need to be seen idling about anywhere near the homeplace. Though he felt bone-tired and numb from hours on his buzzing and bumping machine, he still had enough adrenalin-driven energy to carry on. Around midnight he got back on the Honda and headed toward the homeplace.

When he reached Ackley, a tiny farm town just outside Black Hawk County, he realized he still had plenty of time. It was almost one in the morning and though there was no traffic, some late night partiers driving home in their Halloween getups might notice a motorcyclist. Halloween was still a big costume night for some adults, going all-out to find zany get-ups. A biker out there on Halloween might be something they'd remember. But tonight, no traffic, and a nearly full moon made the countryside glow blue-white.

As he neared Finchford, he pulled off on a gravel road to complete preparations. He parked in the darkness and got out his tiny flashlight. He opened the luggage box, retrieved his tennis shoes, revolver, and cartridges. He took off his riding boots, pulled on his sneakers, counted six cartridges and loaded them into the cylinder, then dropped a handful of loose cartridges into his denim jacket. He figured he would need to reload, maybe more than once. He lay the loaded revolver on top of his camping gear and other clothes and snapped the lid shut. If he were picked up now he would have serious explaining to do, so he took his time, watching for traffic and riding as slowly and quietly as he could back onto the highway.

He glanced at his watch: 2:30 in the morning.

6: The Marks' Halloween

LES AND JORJEAN MARK seldom disagreed, but the last day of October they found themselves at odds. Jorjean wanted to take Jeff and Julie out in full costumes for trick-or-treating, but Les said no, they shouldn't eat so much candy, he was too busy with the harvest to bother, and it was a dumb custom anyway. The young husband didn't believe that last point, but he wanted to appeal to his wife's rebel nature. She combined love of tradition and custom with an occasional offbeat surprise. He loved that about her.

Jorjean pointed out over breakfast that the kids loved Halloween, and hilarious snapshots of their goofy costumes made it a highlight of their year. Besides, it was only once a year. "Don't be a Halloween Scrooge," she needled him. But he refused to budge and reminded her that last year Jeff had thrown up. Neither child had slept all night, nor had they.

Jorjean remembered, and admitted that last Halloween turned out to be a nightmare, with two wide-awake sick kids. Julie and Jeff seemed to have a gift for wolfing down bags of the stuff before anyone could stop them.

After Les left for another harvest day, Jorjean thought better of it. The guy was probably right, she mused, as she washed breakfast dishes. Harvest was exhausting enough, and running around the neighborhood in costume would wear them out. A sure recipe for heavy stress, she decided, so resolved to agree with Les and skip the costumes and trick-or-treating after all.

Jeff stayed restless and whiny all day, so she resolved not to say anything to him about Halloween. When the sitter brought Julie back from preschool, the little girl launched a barrage of questions. She had seen all the other preschool kids' excitement and it was contagious. Julie was a typical five-year old—all energy and questions, ready for anything that looked fun, and seemed to love their animals and even helping with the chores.

"Mommy, when are we going trick-or-treating tonight? Will we go to all the neighbors or can we go into town? What can I wear? Can I go as a ghost or a witch?"

Jeff picked up her excitement, and the siblings jumped and raced around the kitchen, chanting "Ghost, ghost, ghost," until Jorjean had to shush them. Then she gave them the bad news.

"Julie and Jeff, I'm sorry, but we're not going trick and treating this year. Your daddy's too busy and we have lots to do tomorrow, so you'll need a good night's sleep. You know you don't sleep when you eat candy."

She hoped that reasoning would carry the day.

"Not fair! We never get to go out with the other kids. Why can't we at least get dressed up?" Julie had learned to whine with the best of them, probably just like she did when she was five, Jorjean thought ruefully. "That's not fair," she came back at Julie. "You know this is the first time we've missed, and we'll go out for sure next year. That's a promise."

Julie didn't look satisfied, but at least she quieted down, and that calmed Jeff. He looked downcast, but wasn't old enough to worry about it for long. Within a few minutes they were outside playing with Toby, shouting and laughing at the little dog's sheer joy at seeing them. He loved them as much as they loved him. Jorjean still felt badly about shutting down the kids' happiest night of the year, but knew Les was right.

Les hadn't been home when she gave them the news and Jorjean was thankful that he hadn't seen their downturned faces. An easy mark for their children's begging, Les had often given in to their whining and complaining. If Les had one flaw, it was his soft spot for his kids' entreaties. Jorjean was the real disciplinarian in their family. Once she made up her mind, she didn't second-guess herself.

The young couple made a pact when Jorjean got pregnant that they would never argue in front of their kids. Both remembered how much they hated seeing their parents argue, so resolved to spare their kids from seeing them bicker. They knew where to set and enforce boundaries for their children, and it worked. Jeff and Julie were often held up as model children by other parents, thanks to their parents' love and spot-on child-rearing instincts.

Les came out of the field late that afternoon. They sat down to a Halloween supper of roast chicken, new potatoes, and green beans from their garden. As they finished, Jorjean served chocolate pudding with one piece of Halloween candy each for dessert. They were one contented, well-fed family.

After dinner Les and Jorjean talked about the harvest, which was going well. In fact it looked large enough to yield extra cash. They both felt good about Les being on the verge of closing two farm sales that would add a sizable sum to their net worth. They talked about brother

Jerry's recent phone call asking Les for a recommendation based on the supposed good work Jerry had done on their farm—after he had moved to Texas, then California. Les had mailed him a newsy "yes" letter the day before, and told Jorjean it was a white lie that might help Jerry find work. He hadn't actually spoken to his brother, but Jorjean had taken the call from Berkeley and had told him that Les would probably agree to it. He was generous like that.

Neither Les nor Jorjean wanted to talk more about family, since wounds that were opened in May still had not healed. Les mentioned that Jerry seemed to be serious about getting his act together, so he was glad to help. Sooner or later Jerry would succeed at something, he told his skeptical wife, but right now he needed to find work. In spite of their differences, Les loved his older brother.

The phone rang, ending their conversation. Jorjean answered, as usual, and Les turned down the TV news. He heard her laughing and greeting "Barb," and knew that her best friend Barbara Wulf had called. Jorjean was nodding and telling Barbara about their kids' disappointment at missing treats and costumes. Then she held her hand over the receiver and whispered to Les, "Do you mind if we go over to Wulfs' for a few minutes? They're grilling steaks and want to give Julie and Jeff some Halloween treats."

Les nodded OK, and realized this was a fair trade-off for not taking them around the neighborhood in costume. Jorjean told Barbara they'd stop by in about an hour, and finished the dishes as Les read the paper. Les relied on the Waterloo *Courier* and the Des Moines *Register* for the news.

Well after 8:00 they headed into Cedar Falls, driving to the Wulf's for a quick visit. Les and Jorjean enjoyed their time with their friends and seldom missed an opportunity to see them. The two couples shared love of kids and a deep attachment to the community through church. Best of all they all loved to drink beer and tell raucous jokes. They formed a natural foursome.

By 9:30 they were back home and settling in for the night. Les left to help finish the day's harvest—it was his busiest time—and Dorothy and Wayne stopped by for a quick goodnight visit. They didn't say long, Wayne tiring quickly. After they left, Les returned, and the little family sat down to late dessert with pudding and Kool-Aid. Jorjean realized it was getting far past the kids' bedtime, so she walked them upstairs, kissed them both lightly on their foreheads as they snuggled down, promising them a better Halloween next year. They both seemed pacified, and quickly fell asleep.

As Jorjean came downstairs she could see their Uncle Victor's Ford pull into their driveway. Les was always glad to see Victor, who worked full-time in town as a city fireman, and helped when he could with the harvest. Victor offered his usual "hallo, you two" and asked what Julie and Jeff had worn for Halloween, and teased them when he learned that the stuffy old parents hadn't bothered with costumes.

Les and Victor both left to haul a few more truckloads of corn from a corn dryer down the road back to their bin on the homeplace farm. They hauled four loads of corn from the dryer to the bin in two different trucks, and didn't quit until well after midnight. Both men were used to never getting quite enough sleep, especially during fall harvest, and both planned an early start the next morning. Les came in again around 12:30, and Uncle Vic finished auguring the last of the corn into the storage bin, leaving around 1:00.

Jorjean was already in bed when Les got into his pajamas, dead-tired from his long day. So tired that he left the downstairs lights on, as he realized when he moved toward their bed. Seeing Jorjean nestled in her baby-blue nightgown in the soft light, he felt a familiar and irresistible rush of love and lust. Les loved Jorjean as the mother of his children and his daily advisor and companion, but he loved her immediately and powerfully as his lifetime lover. They enjoyed a rich and imaginative sex life, which both relaxed and bonded them.

In spite of his fatigue, his desire for Jorjean took over, and he flipped on the bedroom light, just to see her wake up. Toby, asleep in his dog bed, looked up with alarm, then relaxed and put his head down, dozing off.

The glaring overhead light startled Jorjean, and she sat up and looked sleepily at her husband. "What's going on? Why all the lights?"

"Just wanted you to know I'm completely in love with you," and he lay down beside her. They kissed, long and deep. Jorjean, barely awake, giggled and pulled him over and on her. They held each other close for a few minutes. They each knew how to pleasure the other, and each gave freely; they both loved how much they enjoyed their physical pleasures. Les dozed lightly, then stirred, climbing into his pajamas, left to turn off the lights, then returned in the dark to cocoon in his wife's arms. The house felt secure and quiet.

It had been a near-perfect day, Jorjean mused as she drifted off —even without the kids' trick-or-treats. The couple fell together into a deep, calm sleep.

7: Intruder

HE CROUCHES IN the ditch, watches and waits. The downstairs lights brighten the yard well past 2:30. After a few minutes he pulls on his gloves, moves to the phone junction box in deep underbrush in the ditch beside the road, slides off the top, clips the phone wires, slips the top back, pockets his cutter. As he backs away he steps into a hole, stumbles, twists his knee and puts out a hand to stop his fall. His jacket flops outward with the motion. Cursing his clumsiness, he gathers his thoughts and crouches, waiting for the house to go dark.

He stays low, moves silently to the pickup camper sitting in the yard beside the barn. Lights from the house help him see enough to make out the table and chairs and cot inside. Empty.

Finally the lights go out. Moving to the back porch, he climbs the stairs, peers into the dark kitchen. He takes the key off the hook, lets himself in, makes his way into the moonlit kitchen. Toby, he remembers, always slept with them in their bedroom.

Slinking noiselessly, he moves through the kitchen into the living room, down a small hallway past their grandfather clock to the cellar stairs near their bedroom. He knows the house well. Aware that the ancient stairway could creak and groan, he creeps down two at a time, careful to step only on the side of each stair. No noise emanates. In the cellar he struggles with whether to smoke, knowing the foreign smell could wake them. But he needs to calm himself. He lights a Marlboro. Shaking, he inhales deeply and slowly, letting the nicotine work. He reads his watch by the cigarette's glow: 2:45.

He crushes the Marlboro out on the cellar floor, lowers his backpack and draws out the loaded revolver wrapped in a towel. He unwraps the gun, grasps it tightly. Breathing deeply and steadily, he listens for sounds. Nothing. The upstairs has stayed quiet since he entered.

He takes a deep breath and moves up the stairs quickly into the living room, his face all but glowing in the dark. It's time.

Gliding to the bedroom door, he turns the knob noiselessly and pushes. Toby jumps up and barks once. He grabs the dachshund-mutt and pulls him outside the bedroom. He slides his hand up the wall, flips on the bedroom ceiling light, its glare floods the room.

Les and Jorjean stir awake from the barking and sudden brightness. Les sits up, groggy, squinting, shading his eyes.

"Hey," he yells. "Hey! What the hell do you think you're doing? Get out of here!"

"Out of the bed and kneel with a pillow on the floor," he shouts. "Hurry up! I'm gonna clean up this family once and for all. You've had your way long enough."

Les grimaces at him, then lunges. He fires a warning round and it cracks into the bedroom floor between Les and his wife. "HOLY SHIT!" Les shouts. "STOP IT! GET THE HELL OUT OF HERE! JESUS CHRIST!"

Jorjean finds her voice. "Whatever you think you're doing won't work. You can't get by with this. Everyone knows… "

"SHUT THE FUCK UP. I don't want to hear another goddamn word out of either of you and I mean it."

"You can't be serious. You… "

Les rears up in bed, and he fires another round between them; this one grazes Jorjean's side. She yells in pain.

"Both of you on the floor, get the fuck on the floor, now!"

With Jorjean wounded and bleeding beside him, Les places his head on the pillow he grabbed from the bed, quickly kneeling on the floor. Jorjean, whimpering in pain, kneels with him.

He moves behind Les and fires twice, both slugs hitting him from behind, above his left ear. Les goes limp, blood immediately running down his neck.

Jorjean screams, shaking and hurting, covers her head with her arms. He moves to his left directly behind her and fires twice into her head. She goes silent and limp, blood flowing from her head.

Shaking, he reloads, pulling cartridges out of his jacket pocket. He fires another round into her back. He body jumps, bleeding heavily.

He swings the revolver again to Les, who lies still on the floor. He fires three more rounds, two into Les's face and another into his stomach. He pushes their bodies aside, and with some effort, pulls the bedroom door open. Les 's body had rolled over to nearly block it. He strides toward the stairway while reloading again.

Upstairs, he finds Julie at the top of the stairs clutching a pillow. She must have heard the shots and came to the top of the stairs to see. She's sleepy but recognizes him. He says nothing, takes her hand and leads her down the hall, opens the door to her bedroom, where she drops her pillow, and he lifts her back into her bed.

"Who's shooting firecrackers?" She looks directly at him. He doesn't speak, but comforts her with a pat on the head. She lies back.

Julie looks directly at him, murmuring, not quite asleep. He struggles with what to do, since she's still looking straight at him. He backs away from the bed so she can't see him, turns around, cups a match and lights a Marlboro. He needs to calm his nerves anyway. He stands quietly in the dark, puffs on the cigarette, relaxes. After a few minutes he looks again and sees she's finally asleep, breathing easily. He drops the half-smoked Marlboro on the bedroom floor, twists it out with his foot and kicks it under her bed.

He points the revolver at her head and fires from barely a foot away. The little girl snaps back hard on her bed, her face suddenly speckled. He aims at her chest and fires again. The little girl's body jumps. Blood begins to stain the bedding around her body.

He moves across the hallway into Jeff's bedroom. Jeff stirs, but stays asleep.

He fires a round directly into the little boy's head, and quickly another into his chest, just as with Julie. One of the bullets exits the bottom of the bed and blows a hole in Jeff's storybook beneath the bed.

Now in a hurry, he all but jumps downstairs, bounds back down into the cellar and pulls the main breaker switch. The electric clock in Les and Jorjean's bedroom stops at 3:05.

He emerges from the cellar into the living room, moves down the hallway and whacks the face of the heirloom grandfather clock hard, three times, with the butt of the revolver, which shatters the glass in both the face and the bottom. He pulls a few desk drawers open from the adjacent office room, littering the floor with papers.

He runs from the kitchen and slams the door behind him. He turns the key, locking the door and replaces the key on the hook. Grabbing a potted fern from the porch table, he heaves it through the back door window, shattering glass and bursting the heavy pot on the kitchen floor, glass and dirt splattering across the linoleum.

Striding, he jumps off the porch steps and breaks into a run for the Honda a few hundred feet away. He shivers; the early November air hovers around forty degrees. The cold comforts him.

Feeling elated and relieved, he starts the bike and steers it west, riding as fast as he dares. No one had seen or heard him, as far as he knew.

8: Discovery

CLARK RENNER, LONG-TIME Mark family helper and friend, drove to the Mark homeplace around 7:00 Saturday morning, expecting to meet Les to start the day's harvesting. Having called the house several times, he was growing impatient. He decided to go bang on their door and rouse the sleepyheads. How could Les still be asleep, he wondered. By now his cheerful neighbor and co-worker should be outside ready to get to work, with the kids and Jorjean bouncing around in the kitchen, waving them goodbye, excited about Saturday, as always. Every Saturday was a holiday for Julie and Jeff.

Though neither Clark nor Les would admit it, they loved their work, the long hours and endless unpredictability of weather, machines, and markets. They both grew up farming; working the soil had become embedded in their character, as had their rituals of complaining about weather, price supports, the price of fuel. They never whined, but loved complaining.

A big man, rotund in a middle-aged way, Renner sported a deeply burnished face and forearms due to constant exposure to Iowa's summer sun. In another time and place, except for girth, he could have modeled for an Andrew Wyeth painting—the stolid farmer set against rolling Iowa cornfields. He parked as usual in the gravel driveway and noticed the house remained dark. And the Marks' corn dryer, which should have been running all night, sat silent.

Odd, he thought. They needed to dry the corn for transport to market. Renner eased himself out of his pickup and walked stiffly to the dryer and tripped its switch. Nothing. Surprised, he toggled it again, but still nothing. Moving to the camper near the barn where Les sometimes slept, he rapped hard, the sound echoing off the barn. No response. By now the house should be brightly lit, humming and bumping with life. Not home? He wondered.

Did one of the kids get sick? Did they rush to the emergency room? Had they stayed over in town? Thoughts begin to churn. Les and Jorjean never slept in, especially during harvest. If nothing else, Julie and Jeff would wake them and they'd be stirring. Maybe they had a long night last night and were just too exhausted to stir. Les and Jorjean loved to celebrate holidays, especially Halloween, with their kids, so maybe they just wore themselves out.

Renner walked around to the south side of the house, peered into the porch. He saw the glass and dirt, an obvious mess. Probably a Halloween prank, he thought, but vandalism was unusual in Iowa, even in isolated farmhouses. He knocked on the outside screen door loudly. Toby barked at his knock, as usual. Renner knocked harder and yelled, "LES—JORJEAN—YOU THERE?" Toby's yips answered, more high-pitched and urgent.

Clearly someone had done some damage here. He could see the fern and its pot scattered in disarray on the kitchen floor. Someone had hurled it through the window. Renner decided to rouse the elder Marks.

It wasn't his place to enter a neighbor's unoccupied house. Within minutes he knocked on Dorothy and Wayne's front door in Turkey Foot Heights while pushing the doorbell. It was well into the 7:00 hour, so Dorothy and Wayne would be stirring. Like Renner, they kept farmers' habits—early-to-bed and early-to-rise. Dorothy came to the door in her housecoat, looking disheveled but wide-awake as always. She was nothing if not intense.

"Clark?" She flipped the porch switch and they both stood in the light. "What in the world? Come in for coffee."

Dorothy Mark was a stout middle-aged woman who carried herself with confidence and aplomb. Graying brown hair set in an old-fashioned bun framed her business-like features. Always quick with opinions, perpetually impatient, she seldom doubted or changed her first impressions. Her face seemed nearly as chiseled and masculine as her husband's, whose features looked hard and worn. A longtime cancer patient suffering from cobalt treatments for a tumor behind his right eye, Wayne Mark still managed to get around, but didn't volunteer information without being asked, and wasn't known for a cheery demeanor. At this point, treatments were palliative rather than curative. Though barely over sixty, anyone would have taken him for closer to seventy.

Renner offered a weak smile that didn't disguise his worry. The Marks never suffered fools gladly, so he explained himself. "Something's happened at the homeplace. Probably just a prank, but I didn't want to go poking around without permission."

"What? What're you talking about?"

"I just drove over to get an early start and everything was turned off, including the augur. I tried to raise Les, but he wasn't in the camper. The house's still dark. Back porch door window's busted out, glass all over the place. I figured I'd better check with you."

"All right, let's get over there. I'm sure they're home. Thanks, Clark—we'll see you there." She felt slightly annoyed at having her early morning so rudely interrupted. She hadn't yet read the front page of the *Register*, a morning ritual.

Renner started back in his truck while Dorothy and Wayne dressed for November air. Within minutes the Marks were following Renner's route south on Union Road to the homeplace, where they had lived for decades until September. It was a short stretch of rural road, barely two miles, and at that time of the year, much of the crop had been gathered. The combines had done their work, cleaning all but a few fields down to stumps of stalks, leaving a bare subsistence ration for crows and deer. By late October it was midwestern tundra.

When they arrived, Renner waved for them to park beside him. Dorothy got out and exclaimed, "Why, they're not even out of bed yet!" Wayne stayed in their pickup truck, unable to walk without daunting effort.

Renner and Dorothy stepped onto the porch and surveyed the damage. Vandals, they assumed, had tossed that heavy fern, pot and all, through the kitchen door window. Dorothy pushed the door open and they stepped into scattered window glass, which crunched and popped. Toby, who recognized them, came wagging, happy to finally have company. They petted him and let him outside. Morning light streamed into the kitchen, and they stepped around the mess into the den. Moving to the east side of the house, they made their way to Les and Jorjean's bedroom. Renner noticed that the grandfather clock in the hallway had been badly smashed, the glass shattered and the face bent. The clock's hands read 3:05. Dorothy clucked her tongue and shook her head as she noticed the vandalized clock.

Les and Jorjean's bedroom door seemed shut tight. Dorothy pushed it but it didn't budge. They looked down. A pool of blood had seeped from under the door and glistened in the morning sunlight.

Dorothy found her voice, exclaiming, "Aww, Clark, look at this!"

Renner stared, unbelieving, holding his breath. His body tensed as his adrenaline surged. The two fell silent, uncomprehending, breathing hard.

"Dorothy, I can't go in there. Call the Sheriff."

"I'll go in." Dorothy pushed harder against the door, which still barely budged. When she managed to crack it slightly, she could see Les's rigid body, then made out both Les and Jorjean curled on the floor in pools of blood. She could see a bullet wound in Jorjean's back, but no other wounds.

"Clark, they've been shot!" She didn't push further into the room or try to look more closely at her youngest son and his wife. She struggled with what to do.

Renner was paralyzed. He had no experience with traumas on this scale. Dorothy finally took charge. "Get down to the basement and flip the breaker. I think the main switch has been tripped."

"Let's find the kids first."

"Oh, yes, oh, oh, my little ones. I hope they slept through whatever happened down here."

They climbed the stairs and walked toward the west hall to five-year-old Julie's bedroom and peered in. Both stood in shock as they gazed at the little girl's body. She had been shot in the chest, and slashed or stabbed on the face, from what they could tell, her face riddled with specks.

Dorothy breathed hard, struggling to speak.

"Julie's dead too. Who could have done this?"

Renner felt waves of nausea, not just from the girl's blood-soaked body and mattress, but from the brutality, the sheer horror he confronted. This was monstrous.

They sensed they shouldn't touch anything and moved unsteadily together down the hallway to Jeff's bedroom. The little boy lay in his blood-soaked bed, large wounds in his face and chest. After a few stunned moments, Dorothy gathered her thoughts and moved toward the stairs.

"My whole family's dead!" she exclaimed, "Someone must have broken in and—and—what will we do?" She steadied herself, took control of her urge to break down.

Renner could not stop shaking. Dorothy knew they had to get busy.

"I'll call the police. You tell Wayne. I should call Jorjean's folks. Power—we need the power on. I'll go down and switch it on."

"Dorothy, I'm so sorry. I'll call Carol." Renner needed his wife, and knew that Dorothy needed help.

He found a phone and managed to dial. Dorothy headed to the basement. Enough light came through to let her see the breaker panel. The main switch had been pulled, and she flipped it on. The house lit up; kitchen lights filled the downstairs, and as Renner walked out the door he heard Dorothy calling the Sheriff.

Dorothy slipped into automatic mode, which kept her going during those first terrible hours.

"Black Hawk County Sheriff? Yes, we need help here. This is Dorothy Mark, and I'm at the Mark Homeplace on Union Road. My son's family has been shot. Four people. Yes, all four… "

Renner walked unsteadily to the pickup where the Mark family patriarch sat, all but dozing. Renner motioned Wayne to roll down the window and, almost gasping, gave him the terrible news.

"Shot? No, no. That can't be. I just saw them yesterday. No one would shoot my boy. Where's Dorothy?"

"She's calling the Sheriff and a doctor. They're on the way."

The old man eased himself out of the truck and made his way into the house. Renner helped him up the back stairs and into the kitchen, where Dorothy stood amidst the scattered glass. "Wayne, even Julie and Jeff."

As her words sank in, Wayne looked stricken, his face contorted. He slumped against the wall. "We know who did this," he muttered, looking hard at his wife.

"Hush, you old fool—just shut up. You don't have any idea. Wait for the Sheriff."

Renner stared at Wayne and then Dorothy, not sure what to say. He sensed a tension between them that had deep roots. Then he headed for the door, wanting air and space. He still felt sick, and resisted an urge to just drive away. It felt ugly and evil. Dorothy and Wayne hardly noticed Renner leave the house. Finally Wayne moved heavily to the den and sank into the sofa, not speaking.

Dorothy kept going. "I'd better call the Colthursts. We'll need Reverend Burris." She walked to the kitchen phone, needing to keep busy. Over the years Dorothy had become a master of busying herself with work, ignoring problems by working harder. It worked for her, as it did for most rooted Midwesterners.

Cars began arriving. Carol Renner arrived just as the sheriff's deputy's car bounced into the driveway, followed closely by the doctor. Soon the Marks' driveway would be filled with police cars and reporters who had been alerted by police radio. They cut across the grass, avoiding approaching the house from the driveway, aware they might trample evidence.

Within an hour, the first investigators had searched for but found no weapon near the bodies. That ruled out murder-suicide. By early afternoon Don Richardson, a local funeral director, had transported the four bodies to the county morgue for autopsy, and by Saturday evening the entire country knew that a family of four had been murdered execution-style in their farm home in rural Black Hawk County near "The Lawn City," Cedar Falls, Iowa.

9: Investigating Begins

"So where do we start?" asked Iowa Bureau of Criminal Investigation (BCI) Assistant Director Tom Ruxlow as he greeted David Dutton, Black Hawk County Attorney, in Dutton's office in the Black Hawk County Courthouse. The office reflected a no-nonsense approach, with state-issue furniture and few wall decorations. Only his desk held a few reminders that he was a family man, with photos of his wife and children featured prominently. Never a man for decorative niceties or small talk, he nonetheless stayed friendly and open. Dutton was both respected and liked, a rare combination of rigor and warmth. Lean, dark haired, handsome, with eyes that never seemed to miss anything, he probably could have become a senator or even governor had he taken up politics. Deeply competitive, Dutton seldom lost at anything, especially difficult criminal cases. Oddly, he remained above the political fray, never openly committing to a party or political cause.

Ruxlow had driven up that morning from BCI Headquarters in Des Moines, and Dutton appreciated his help. In fact, he would come to value assistance from a variety of police agencies, including the Waterloo police, the Black Hawk County Sheriff's office, the State BCI, and several other law enforcement agencies in states along Interstate 80 across the country as they learned of the brutal murders. He also came to count on Assistant County Attorneys David Correll and Harry Zanville. Correll helped with field investigations and operated as a liaison with Dutton's office, and Zanville did the extensive legal research upon which they built their case. They devoted all their energy and time to solving this case. David Dutton stayed fully in charge, but he relied on both Correll and Zanville for logistics and details. Ruxlow made sure everything got done. The four of them made a formidable investigative cohort.

All of them took the Mark murders downright personally. Investigators and officers alike struggled with the execution-style coldness of the crime and the inhumanity of killing children in their beds. All of them were haunted by the illustrated children's book *I am a Bunny*, which they found under Jeff's bed. The bullet had passed through the boy, his mattress, then through the book and into the floorboard.

This was no ordinary murder case. Many of them worked nights and weekends without compensation; in those days, no one received overtime pay. They figured the long hours came with the territory.

Tom Ruxlow related preliminary reports from on-site investigators. Known for his dry wit and ready smile, "Rux" possessed a talent for remembering facts and names as well as a sharp analytical intelligence. He had been promoted quickly within the Cedar Falls Police Department. He later accepted a position as an agent with the Iowa Bureau of Criminal Investigation and went on to become director. His co-workers respected and liked his rare combination of hard driving and soft speaking. He held his considerable size well, lumbering as much as walking, but never seemed clumsy. In fact, he had excelled in both track and football in high school, and kept himself in decent shape.

The two men planned a series of meetings with local police and sheriff's deputies. This case would fully engage both men and dozens of investigators for months. By Sunday evening Dutton and company had set up an investigative command center in the county courthouse, taking over a small suite of adjoining offices.

"OK, Rux—what do we know?"

"It wasn't a murder-suicide. And we're pretty sure it wasn't a robbery. Nothing of any real value's missing. We're looking at someone who knew the place pretty well. The main breaker was pulled, and the killer seemed to know his way around the house, or at least used a flashlight to find his way."

"Were phone lines cut?"

"Yes and no. The lines across the road on an almost-hidden phone box were snipped, but they didn't connect to the Mark house. The wires in that box hooked up to the neighbors' phones, but until a few months ago ran to the Mark's." Ruxlow had just talked to a deputy who had found the cut lines in a ditch in the underbrush. They knew Dorothy had called the Sheriff from the homeplace phone, so that line was working. She had told the deputy about the phone junction boxes being changed. John Jutte, a BCI agent, found two live .38 caliber cartridges near the junction box while inspecting the cut lines.

Dutton responded, "How about that. So it might have been someone who thought they knew more than they knew."

"Yeah. And we found footprints out by the camper and around to the door to the kitchen. Les sometimes slept in the camper, according to Clark Renner, Les's helper. I know Renner, by the way." Ruxlow had worked in Cedar Falls as a lieutenant on the police department before he joined the BCI, so knew many of the people they were dealing with.

Dutton continued. "We need fingerprints. How's that going?"

"Good. They're dusting everything. No luck so far. We're finding cigarette butts. No casings. We'll know what caliber this afternoon. Probably .38, given those live cartridges in the ditch."

Dutton, who knew little about weapons, asked, "Hmm, how many were fired?"

"Not sure. We've found several slugs, and the autopsies will show more. The Marks were all shot more than once. Deputies are searching the property for anything he might have left behind."

"He? Or they? Or she?"

Dutton speculated. "Well, who knows? I'd like to think that no woman would murder kids like that. We're probably not looking at some random killings or a burglary." Both men were old school, believing that women were mostly incapable of serious violence, especially to children.

Ruxlow had investigated plenty of homicides, and knew that close family members needed to be cleared first. Burglars tried to avoid confrontations, which could lead to assault or even murder raps. What burglar or random drifter would have sought out and killed two kids in their upstairs bedrooms, shooting at point-blank range? It looked to him more like someone "cut off a limb from the family tree," as he put it. That meant family might very well be involved. He had surveyed the scene himself that morning, as had Dutton. Disturbing. So much violence in such a confined space. They couldn't shake mental images of the bloody, lifeless children.

"So who's related to Les Mark around here?" Dutton asked, ready to make calls.

10. The Mark Brothers

RUXLOW KNEW THE FAMILY. "Well, there's Tom. You might know him—usually in some kind of mix-up around town. A bit off-balance."

"Yeah, let's interview him right away. Aren't there other brothers? Who's the oldest?"

"I think that would be Richard, then Jerry, then Tom. Les was the youngest."

"Good. How'd you know all this?" Dutton liked Ruxlow. No chit-chat or gossip.

"I lived in Cedar Falls when these guys were growing up. This morning I talked to Rev. Burris, who's with Dorothy and Wayne now. He thought we should get Tom in soon. Dorothy agreed."

"OK, let's find all the brothers, then look at other relatives. Let's look for anyone who might have hated Les or Wayne for whatever business dealings." Both men had dealt with crimes committed by angry business associates and clients and knew that revenge for a deal gone sour wasn't out of the question.

Dutton mulled over his mental images of the crime scene. He had viewed the bodies before the funeral director transported them to the morgue. He wasn't newly minted, but he had never seen anything like this. Those shot-up corpses stayed with him as motivation. Nobody deserved a fate like that, least of all those good people. Utterly violated, he thought to himself.

Ruxlow interrupted his thoughts. "I think brother Dick lives and preaches in Canada. And Jerry's living in California, separated from his wife. We've been trying to reach him since Saturday, but no luck. I'm sure they'll all be here for the funeral by early next week. That only leaves Tom. He lives in downtown Waterloo and hangs around bars and strip clubs. We'll get him in as soon as we can pick him up. That's the best we can do."

Dutton knew that people wouldn't stand for a stalled investigation in a multiple murder case. "When's the funeral, Rux?"

"I think it's Tuesday afternoon at the United Methodist Church in Cedar Falls. Going to be huge. Everyone knows the Mark family. We'll have people there."

Dutton mentioned that he had talked to Dorothy late that morning, and she seemed remarkably composed. He knew the Marks and spoke to them on a first-name basis. "I told her not to worry, that we would find whoever did this. She said all the neighbors are scared out of their holy skins."

Ruxlow laughed. "That's Dorothy, all right. She's tough, and she'll help us. God, to lose your kids and grandkids that way."

"Who knows what kind of psycho we've got out there. Let's get some leads."

Dutton sat down hard behind his desk, his thoughts tumbling. Who the hell would do this? With these monstrous murders, anything was possible.

The next-to-youngest Mark brother lived by himself in a downtown Waterloo hotel, frequenting bars and seedy hangouts. Not a neer-do-well, he was more of a never-well, having been diagnosed at first as an alcoholic, then a schizophrenic—a debilitated man.

Dorothy suggested to friends that "his thoughts get ahead of his mind," meaning he regularly lapsed into incoherence. In fact, his whole life seemed incoherent—nothing he did fit with anything else. He couldn't be depended upon for anything. Not work, not friendship, not even keeping track of the old Chevy, which by now was sitting at the homeplace waiting to be sold or junked.

By Sunday afternoon investigators had found Tom in downtown Waterloo and brought him in. Tom, never quite sure what to do, asked them to call Bill Sindlinger, the Mark family lawyer. Sindlinger told Tom that he couldn't represent him. The lawyer knew that he would be representing the elder Marks' interests, and wouldn't be able to defend Tom with any impartiality. Given Tom's reputation, he was in fact a potential suspect.

Dutton and Ruxlow told Tom that he had a right to stop answering questions at any time and they would find him another lawyer, so he agreed to answer questions. Where was he, then, on Halloween night? Tom, who couldn't remember much, told them that he slept off and on all day, ate a hamburger at a local bar, then walked to a downtown strip club. Later he returned to his hotel room and slept.

He also mentioned that he had never owned or fired a gun. They noticed that Tom didn't really understand what had happened to brother Les and his family. Nor did he know that Les, Jorjean, and their kids had moved to the homeplace several weeks before. He thought they still lived at the Cedar Mark farm a few miles west. Tom wasn't able to make sense out of the questions, much less answer them.

When Dutton and Ruxlow heard Tom's replies, along with his inability to focus, they took him off the list. No way, they knew, could he plan and commit such a crime, or any crime, except accidentally. These murders were anything but accidental. Just to keep him around for more questioning, they put him in the county lockup.

Tom agreed to let them search his hotel room, and that search confirmed their suspicion. They found nothing of interest, and to be safe, they took his clothes for close examination and found only a few sand burrs that he had picked up when walking down a railroad track in Waterloo.

"OK," said Ruxlow. "What about Richard?" He and Dutton were having coffee in Dutton's office after another briefing with both local police investigators.

"Coming from Canada—Dick and his wife both. They haven't lived in Iowa for years. Visits on holidays, that's about it."

"What's he do?"

"He works for a religious organization of some kind. Ordained. I think he married Les and Jorjean back in 1970 and probably will give the eulogy at the funeral. He never took much interest in Iowa or farming. Dorothy and Wayne seem proud of his religious career."

"OK, so we can interview him along with the folks tomorrow. Down at Sindlinger's office." Dutton nodded a yes to that. The Mark family would prefer their lawyer's familiar office to police interrogation rooms. Besides, they would appreciate having Sindlinger handy.

Then Dutton asked, "What's with Jerry? When's he coming in?"

"Not sure. They tried to reach him all day yesterday, but no luck. He's probably cruising around California with no itinerary. As soon as they reach him he'll fly back here. Monday night or Tuesday morning at the latest."

"Let's interview Jerry as soon as they find him. We need to move on this."

"OK, I'll call a detective wherever they find Jerry and tell him what we're looking for."

"Great. Then we can eliminate another brother."

11: Ride West

A LONG, MISERABLE RIDE awaited Jerry Mark that early November morning and he felt even more thankful for No-Doz, not to mention surging adrenalin. Fatigue became his major adversary.

His leg hurt from that stumble in the ditch and his right hand was bleeding from a cut across the knuckle, but it could have been worse. Guns always made him nervous. Lucky he didn't get hurt using the damned thing. Les was a strong guy who might have done damage had he been wide awake and warned by an intruder's noise. His brother probably hesitated because he couldn't believe his eyes.

He kept the 450's motor at a steady pace as he eased south to Highway 20 running west. To make real time, he needed to get to Interstate 35, then down to I-80 heading west. He would get the news from Mimi or his mother soon enough, and needed to get far from Iowa. No need to panic and speed.

Now he needed to dump that revolver, the leftover cartridges, tennis shoes, pliers, and eventually his sweatshirt, though he would like to keep it for warmth until he absolutely had to ditch it. He also had to get that Iowa plate off and dump it, probably after he got out of Nebraska. He would leave the other cutting pliers in the tool kit.

He knew that if he were stopped and searched now, he'd be dead meat. He wasn't sure what he would do. Shoot the cop? Hardly. Try to outrun him? Hardly again. He'd have to give up and talk fast, and that sure as hell wouldn't work. He'd just have to be careful and hope for dumb luck. Even if they found something suspicious they could never place him at the homeplace. He had a story and he was going to stick to it.

He now faced the most risky part—getting the hell away just when fatigue could overwhelm him into making stupid mistakes. He turned off the main rural road and took a one-lane gravel road to a wooded wetland. He found a narrow entrance, barely visible from the road. With no time to search for a perfect hideaway, he felt thankful that the harvest moon yielded enough light to reveal a large hole—maybe a fox's den or woodchuck burrow, and shoved the revolver, tennis shoes, pliers, cartridges, box and all, as deep into the hole as he could reach, jammed it further in with a small log, then packed the hole shut and threw brush over it and fluffed it around. Some burrows go down several feet and can't be seen even when looking right at them.

He figured they would never find that stuff unless they fanned out for miles and covered every square foot with metal detectors. He had already ridden miles from the homeplace. He knew he had outwitted them.

He kicked the Honda hard, riding as fast as he dared. He knew that they would try to find him—relatives, cops, everyone—with the news, so he ought to call Mimi, play dumb, and keep heading toward California until he could make the alibi stick. But he couldn't do that until he rode well into Nebraska with no calls and no witnesses. He took another No-Doz, thoughts spinning.

Pegging the bike just above the speed limit, he felt confident that few cops were patrolling rural two-lanes. Later he would reconnect the odometer. He wouldn't need gas until he got to I-35.

Though he knew he was in no danger of an emotional meltdown, an image arose unbidden several times. In Les and Jorjean's bedroom, he could still make out the look on Les's face when he fired the first shot. Disbelief, anger, fear, reflecting "How could you?" Les must have felt like Caesar when he saw Brutus coming at him. Damn, he hadn't counted on an attack of conscience.

Jerry had probably always been a borderline sociopath, something he would never admit. He actually enjoyed not having much of a conscience, since he could get by mostly on charm. He had lied his way out of jams with soulful sincerity and pleading, and figured that yokel cops and lawyers weren't smart enough to catch him unless they found hard evidence. He had cultivated being a model citizen, a friend, and an all-around likeable fellow and that had always done the trick.

If necessary, lots of old friends would serve as character witnesses, as would his dear old mom and dad. Since he had just committed the perfect crime, that wouldn't be necessary. But still.

He knew it would take over an hour to get to I-35, gas up, then down to I-80 past Des Moines, then haul ass into Nebraska. He hoped to call Mimi before noon, but avoid telling her his real location. Well before November's first dawn, he rolled into the Boondocks truck stop in Williams, Iowa, on I-35. He stayed with the bike while the young attendant ambled out of the main store/station with the usual "Fill 'er up?"

"Yeh," said Jerry coldly, not wanting to look like he was in a hell of a hurry. The attendant filled it, then pulled the nozzle out of the tank too quickly and splashed gas on the tank. Jerry couldn't help himself, "You sons of bitches don't know how to do anything right." The young guy looked rattled, but didn't reply. Jerry handed the attendant the exact amount—no tip, no change, no thanks—and climbed back on.

As he rolled down I-35, Jerry knew that he had just violated his invisibility rule. Well, he couldn't worry about every little screw-up. Those attendants really were a sorry bunch of guys, he mused, riding another hour south before he could turn west on I-80.

He rode around Des Moines as the sky lightened, then pushed west until he almost dozed off. His mind went unfocused, his legs and back cramped and aching. He rode into a Kwik-Trip and eased off the Honda, suffering from muscle fatigue and back strain. His tailbone felt like it was on fire. He remembered he had cut his hand, so kept his gloves on. He realized that he hadn't kept them on at the first stop. Screwed up again.

He did recall that he had favored his right leg and tried to disguise his limp as he ambled into the station. He still liked Twinkies, a pint of chocolate milk and a hot dog for quick energy and protein, and cheap to boot. He didn't talk to anyone, and didn't want to stop again in Iowa. It was still early morning and he could maybe get into Wyoming before he'd call Mimi.

Jerry began feeling faint, and thought he better sit a few minutes and shut his eyes. He asked the woman behind the counter about the next rest stop. "Ten miles down the road," she said without looking at him, and he took off. In no time he was dozing lightly in a warm toilet stall in the men's room, and in a few minutes shook awake and made himself mount up and roll into Nebraska. Had he not taken more No-Doz, he would have been dead asleep, unable to awaken for hours.

By mid-morning he cruised past Omaha, aware he needed gas again. The low-capacity Honda gas tank was the only bad thing about the 450. Though he felt thankful for the snooze breaks, he needed to get further west fast. He stopped for a quick fill, and took off. As he buzzed along I-80 he remembered that he hadn't checked the Honda's oil since before Ackley, Iowa, so he'd better stop before the next fill. He could tell the machine was burning oil. He rode on awhile and pulled off in Aurora, Nebraska for a top-off and an oil check. A young lone attendant, Mark Van Housen, helped him check the oil, and sold him a quart of oil. Because he didn't use the whole quart, Jerry wanted to carry the leftover with him. He and Van Housen looked for a suitable container. All they could find was an old beer bottle, in which they poured the rest of the oil, stuffed it with a rag, and Jerry stowed it in the luggage box. He took his time—and didn't worry about Van Housen getting a good look at him. After all, he had driven over six hours and nearly 400 miles since he had left the homeplace, and the further he got, the less he worried. He really had outsmarted them.

The gas station in Aurora didn't have a working pay phone, so he left and stopped some 35 miles further west at Alda to call Mimi. He knew he really couldn't tell her where he was—still too close to Iowa, but at least he might get word of the murders. He wondered whether they had started investigating. He felt like an observer, sure he would only play a minor role as Iowa's Keystone Cops scurried about, bouncing off each other. He also knew he couldn't screw up again.

Around 1:30 Jerry dialed Mimi from near Alda, Nebraska, some 35 miles west of Aurora. He wouldn't tell her where he was, just that he wasn't going to get home for the Halloween party that night. He called their Berkeley apartment first. No answer.

Shit, he thought. Maybe I'll just wait a whole day. No, that would seem odd. He decided to call Mimi's parents collect, hoping to reach Mimi. Evelyn, Mimi's mother, tried to answer, but when the operator told him that Mimi wasn't on the line, he refused the call. Evelyn could tell he was still on the line, so she asked, "Jerry, where are you? Call home!"

"I can't say," he answered, and the operator cut them off, since no one agreed to pay charges.

Evelyn knew that her daughter, not her, should tell Jerry the terrible news, but Mimi had not yet arrived from Berkeley. And there was no way they could reach him again. She hoped Jerry would call Iowa and learn it from his own folks.

She talked to her husband Russell about what they should do. He decided to call the police, thinking they could locate Jerry. They both worried that Alga's revolver was missing from Mimi and Jerry's Berkeley storage shed, and that looked bad. In their heart of hearts, they worried that Jerry might actually be implicated in the murders.

Cruising west, Jerry grew more upset with himself. What the hell kind of answer was "I can't say?" Good grief, why not just lie and say "near Cheyenne," which is exactly where he would be by nightfall. A screw-up, he thought, and wondered if he really should just find a rest stop and sleep. He couldn't call again. He would have to say that he thought "call home" meant Berkeley, but he figured correctly that Mimi was probably headed toward her folks' house. She relied on her parents for support whenever she had trouble.

He kept a steady course toward Cheyenne, a good seven or eight hours further with breaks. He would try to hitch a ride in Cheyenne, maybe over to Utah or even Nevada somewhere. He was utterly ex-hausted now, having missed one whole night's sleep, and wasn't sure he could make it to Wyoming without dozing off and killing himself. The day stayed cold and clear, probably in the high thirties with bright sun all day, and he stopped at least twice for naps and gas, plus more hot dogs and chocolate milk. All in all, he felt satisfied that he done all he could, and was home free.

Trying and failing to reach Mimi, he finally gave up. He figured he'd call her from Utah or Nevada, depending on how far he could hitch a ride with his motorcycle in some trailer or other.

He buzzed past Chappell in western Nebraska and dared not stop because the timing was way off now. Around 9:30 Saturday night he arrived at the Little America Truck Stop near Cheyenne, downright desperate for a warm ride.

Steering the Honda near the back of one of the outbuildings, he got out his toolkit. That Iowa plate had to be dumped. Though he needed the sweatshirt for one more ride, the Iowa tag stuck out like a November sunburn. He turned the bolts, eased it off. Behind him sat a large dumpster that was filled with gas station and restaurant waste, probably close to getting emptied and hauled to a landfill somewhere near Cheyenne. He hauled out a half-gallon milk carton, stuffed the plate into it, pinched it tightly shut, and shoved it under a pile of cans and bottles. He pulled out the California tag and bolted it on, making sure he went unseen.

He walked unsteadily to the main café and wondered how in the hell he could get a ride into Utah or Nevada and use it as part of his story. He had parked not far from a North American moving van, and noticed that the driver was climbing into his cab, ready for the road.

He approached the big Freightliner cab and waved hello. The driver rolled down his window. "Hi, bud. What can I do for you?"

"Any way I could hitch a ride with my motorcycle for a ways? I need to get to California soon and I'm not sure I can keep going with the weather so cold."

"Sorry, can't help you. Regulations, and no room back there for a bike. But I was talking to a guy in the café who's hauling an empty horse trailer. He's sitting at the end of the counter, this side. Seemed like a nice guy, and you can probably get your bike hauled in his trailer."

Jerry thought he had hit the jackpot. An empty trailer, a warm cab, and an alibi. "Great," he exclaimed.

This could be too good to be true, Jerry thought as he limped into the café. Sure enough, at the counter sat his Good Samaritan finishing a dessert. "Hi," he said, "That driver said you might be OK with me hitching a ride. I could pay you for gas and keep you company for awhile. I need to get to California as soon as possible, and I'm just too tired to ride my bike."

The horse-hauler, Larry Rauch, looked him over, judged him OK, and kept the conversation going. "Hi, yeah, I'm taking this trailer to Seattle to haul horses back to Iowa. We can push your bike back there and I can get you a good ways by tonight."

Jerry was elated. "Great. I'll just grab a bite here and we can load it up."

By midnight they were rolling down I-80, the Honda secured in the horse trailer, Jerry feeling downright elated. He could rest, doze, talk, and make sure this guy knew his story about staying in Chappell and turning back to California this morning. Now it was just a matter of picking up the pieces and celebrating.

Rauch and Jerry talked freely for awhile, and Rauch later told investigators everything he could—what Jerry was wearing, what they talked about, where and when he dropped him off, what he thought about him. Nothing in his testimony would cause suspicions, since Jerry made sure everything he said and did corroborated his full story. The trucker did remember that the Honda license was from California, and that Jerry wore what appeared to be a hooded sweatshirt.

As November 2nd dawned, Rauch and Jerry pulled into another Little America truck stop near Rock Springs, Wyoming, some 260 miles past Cheyenne. Rauch had originally offered to get Jerry at least to Rock Springs, but Jerry said he would be happy to ride in the truck further, toward Salt Lake City, where Rauch had to turn north. He wanted to luxuriate in the warm cab as long as possible.

Jerry continued to doze and chat amiably, so much so that Rauch later gave Jerry his business card and told him to look him up. Rauch remembered that Jerry never mentioned Iowa. Nor did he ask about finding a phone.

By 8:00 Sunday morning, they had driven to the outskirts of Salt Lake City. Jerry knew he had to continue on I-80, and his horse hauler buddy needed to head north toward Seattle. He had to call Mimi, explain where he was so they could plan what came next.

Jerry thanked Rauch for the ride, and backed the Honda out of the horse trailer. By 8:30 he was riding again, exhausted but elated that he had gotten so far so fast without having to vibrate on the Honda. He realized that he had reached his physical limits before his lucky truck ride.

He figured he could get across Utah and into Nevada by around noon, get rid of his sweatshirt and ride from there. Maybe even back to Berkeley. Dozing and relaxing in Rauch's pickup had energized him. He knew that the trucker would bolster his alibi.

He needed gas again—Honda engineers just couldn't have put a bigger tank on there, could they—and pulled into a station at some no-name town southwest of Salt Lake City and topped it off. He stopped at the smallest, most out-of-the-way station he could find, waved to the attendant to fill it up, and strolled casually around back, out of sight, and found a dumpster that hadn't been emptied in weeks, pulled off his sweatshirt, and stuffed it underneath a pile of oily rags. He made sure it looked like another oily rag by pouring a couple of ounces of motor oil on it from a near-empty bottle.

Paying the rather vacant attendant, he rode back to I-80, feeling lighter and happier than he had for hours. Got rid of that incriminating sweatshirt, got a full tank, got the freedom to ride, he thought, and couldn't help but grin again. What was that line from Janis Joplin? "Freedom's just another word for nothin' left to lose… " he hummed as he clipped along toward Nevada.

Around 1:30 Sunday he stopped in Utah to call Mimi. He found a rest stop with a pay phone away from the main rest area. He knew he was going to need some privacy.

Jerry called their number in Berkeley. No answer. Where the hell was she on a Sunday afternoon? Did she stay over at her mom's in Tahoe? He called the Callenbergs, station to station collect. Mimi's mother answered.

"Hi Evelyn. I'm still trying to reach Mimi. Is she there?"

"No, she should be back at your place now in Berkeley. But Jerry, we've been hoping to hear from you since yesterday, and I didn't get a chance to tell you then. There's terrible news. You have to get home right away."

"What? What are you talking about? I've just been cruising in Utah and Nevada, heading back today. What news?"

"Jerry, your brother Les, Jorjean, and the two kids have been murdered. Someone broke in on Halloween night and shot them all. You have to get back." Evelyn's voice was tremulous, and Jerry audibly gasped. He paused, not sure what he should say first. "NO," he blurted. "WHAT? There's got to be a mistake. Not possible!"

"It's true, Jerry. They're all gone. They've started the investigation and the police are looking for you."

Jerry was taken aback at that comment, but let it go. "Evelyn, is Mimi in Berkeley now?"

"Yes, she should be. You should call her, and get home."

Jerry knew he had to talk to Mimi immediately, so he hung up, upset that they were looking for him so soon. What was that all about?

He called Mimi in Berkeley again, and this time she answered. Finally, he thought.

"Mimi, I just talked to your Mom. What in God's name happened in Iowa? You know all about it?"

"Yes, Jerry. I'm so, so sorry. I can't imagine who would have wanted to do anything like that. They were wonderful people… " She could hear Jerry crying, and didn't know what else to say.

"Jerry, you need to get over to Dad and Mom's place in South Lake Tahoe. I'll meet you there and we can decide what to do. Don't call your parents until you rest up. I've already talked to them, and you can call them tonight from my folks."

Jerry mumbled agreement, sobbed openly, and hung up.

He snapped out of his grief and remembered Evelyn's comment that the police were looking for him. He couldn't help himself; he had to know more. Was he a suspect already? At the next exit he found another phone, called, and Evelyn explained that they were worried about finding him, since he wasn't reachable, so he needed to get back to Iowa fast. He thanked her, cried more, hung up, and headed toward Nevada.

Jerry's head swirled with thoughts of new beginnings as he met Mimi and her father Russell Sunday evening at a restaurant in Carson City, Nevada. Feeling a rush of relief when he hugged Mimi, he hung on to her and sobbed, knowing she could make all the difference. He shook his future father-in-law's hand, gripping it firmly and nodding at the needed condolences. Now he could relax, grieve properly, and move on. Mimi thought he looked terrible, and their first hug chilled her to the bone.

12: Callenberg Call

EARLIER THAT SAME SUNDAY, Mimi's father made a local call to Detective Edwin Newman in South Lake Tahoe and mentioned that his daughter might have information they needed about the Mark murders. The crime had hit the national news late Saturday.

"I'm listening."

"Well, my daughter had a revolver in her possession that disappeared last week."

"OK, and how does this connect to the murders?"

"She's been living with the brother of the Iowa farmer who was killed."

"And where is this brother now?"

"She's not sure. Somewhere around the Mojave Desert, she thinks, on a motorcycle."

"And the revolver?"

"Don't know. She thinks they put it in a storage shed outside their apartment in Berkeley. Somebody broke into it last week."

The detective thanked Callenberg and called the Waterloo Police Department.

13: November 3rd Interview

NEWMAN WAS REFERRED to a Waterloo police detective, who requested that he interview Jerry Mark as soon as possible after Jerry arrived in South Lake Tahoe. Newman knew he needed to gather information on Jerry's whereabouts. The Iowa authorities were trying to eliminate potential suspects as quickly as possible.

"He's not under suspicion, but find out where he was," said the detective. "He'll probably have a story that lets him off the hook. Let's just be sure."

Newman agreed to get a full statement.

He called the Callenbergs and asked if he could talk to Leslie Mark's brother the next morning. Evelyn explained that Mimi and her father were meeting Jerry in Carson City and he was following them back to South Lake Tahoe on his motorcycle, since he didn't know the way. They would arrive later that evening.

"Sure, come ahead," she told Newman. "Jerry will see you in the morning." Completely cooperative, thought Newman. That's a good sign. He wondered whether he should interview Jerry and Mimi together or separately. Since they weren't suspects, he dismissed that thought as arising from his suspicious mind.

That morning Russell Callenberg welcomed Detective Newman. Evelyn, a high school teacher, had already gone to work in South Lake Tahoe. Nice people, he could tell, and obviously concerned about their daughter.

Jerry and Mimi walked into the living room holding hands. As they sat on lounge chairs facing Newman, both seemed to want to help. That pleased the detective. He knew nothing more tedious than interviewing people who hated cops. This couple talked comfortably and easily, even after he turned on his recorder. Jerry was the soul of glibness, though obviously a man in mourning, struggling at times to hold back tears.

Newman liked Mimi immediately. He saw her as a pretty, self-contained young woman who looked and sounded intelligent, who would turn heads wherever she went. Jerry seemed self-assured, polite, cleaned up, and red-eyed from fatigue and grief, Newman supposed. Being an observer by profession, he noticed a fresh cut on Jerry's right hand running diagonally on his index finger over to his second knuckle, about an inch long. It looked like it needed a bandage, but it probably wouldn't stick given the angle and placement.

Neither Jerry nor Mimi had adopted the hippie style, he observed. Mimi wore a dark skirt, white blouse, and low heels. Jerry wore a pair of clean jeans, what looked to be borrowed leather shoes, and a button-down preppy blue shirt, probably that Mimi had brought him from their apartment in Berkeley. To Newman, neither seemed capable of anything like criminal activity, though her father's phone call had alerted him to that missing weapon. So the detective felt an undercurrent of suspicion and interest that he probably would not have felt without that phone call.

Newman hoped to learn Jerry's whereabouts over the weekend, then get on to other, more pressing cases. Mimi, he figured, was just along for the ride, though she might know more than she was letting on. Most spouses and girlfriends did, torn between truth and protective love.

Newman asked Jerry when he first heard the terrible news. Jerry said he called the Callenbergs on Saturday, and Evelyn told him to "call home" right away, but he thought that meant Mimi in Berkeley, not his parents in Cedar Falls. He hadn't called Iowa "home" for years. So he didn't think much about it, other than worrying about Mimi being upset for missing a Halloween party that Saturday night. Newman detected a bit of impatience with Mimi when Jerry spoke about that party, as if she really didn't worry about missing such silly things. She probably did the heavy lifting in their relationship, he thought, though Jerry would certainly insist otherwise.

"I was upset," Jerry told the detective, "because I couldn't seem to reach Mimi on Saturday, so I kept riding west, trying to call her occasionally. Then I called her mom again on Sunday. That's when she told me the godawful news, and said I should ride here as soon as possible to meet Mimi." Jerry grew more agitated as he explained getting that call and having to abruptly change his plans. Newman understood Jerry's off-the-charts stress level, but they all knew that the investigation needed to get family interviews first. Jerry insisted to Newman that he wanted to help catch the killer more than anyone. He even mentioned that his family would put up a substantial reward. They would help catch the bastard, he said, red-faced and angry.

Jerry went on to tell Newman that he rode straight to Carson City, Nevada, where he met Mimi and her dad, then followed them to South Lake Tahoe, arriving late Sunday night. The two of them planned to return to Berkeley that day, and fly to Iowa Monday night for the funeral. Meanwhile, he would leave his Honda with the Callenbergs for safekeeping.

Newman didn't detect as much outright grieving from either of them as he would have expected, but different people react to news of sudden death differently, as he well knew. He empathized; a terrible darkness had descended on this poor family. He felt especially sorry for Mimi, who seemed victimized by circumstances beyond her control.

Jerry offered Newman the story of his trip. He had left Berkeley, Wednesday, headed down toward the Mojave desert, called Mimi from Coalinga, stayed in Southern California near Barstow, and woke up early Thursday feeling downright euphoric. As he put it, "it was a beautiful thing because there was a little bird chirping right by my sleeping bag and the little bird couldn't have been more than just a few feet from me—it was a weird experience, but that woke me up and I felt real good and it was a beautiful day—and so I was really carefree—having a lark, you know." Newman wondered whether the bird was in fact a literal lark, but kept that to himself. Newman couldn't stand smart-ass comments, even witty ones.

He had interviewed hundreds of guilty and innocent folks, and had gotten good at separating the bullshit from the beef, as he put it. He knew too that his bullshit detector wasn't always reliable, so he didn't get too upset with Jerry, and certainly not accusatory, since one lie doesn't mean anything. Hell, we all lie, for all kinds of reasons, he thought. Still, he remembered that moment as the first inkling that Jerry might be spinning.

Then more such moments occurred, and Newman began keeping a mental tally. So polite, so concerned, so ready with answers.

Example: Jerry went on to say that after hearing that cheerful little bird chirping away early Thursday morning, he took off for Vegas, having slept only three hours.

"Off the Five, over to I-15?" Newman asked. "Yes," Jerry admitted, remembering he had hit the California freeways. After only three hours sleep? That seemed like a stretch.

Newman knew that I-80, the major interstate that connects San Francisco and New York, would be Jerry's road of choice to get to Iowa fast. Yet I-80 was nowhere near Coalinga, and Vegas itself sat hundreds of miles southeast of Berkeley and I-80. So how did Jerry get from down by Vegas clear up to I-80? Newman remained unclear on that, and Jerry never explained it to his satisfaction. Sure enough, all of the locations he then mentioned, from Nevada to Nebraska, sat directly on the venerable old interstate: Salt Lake City, Provo, Cheyenne, Chappell.

Another example: Jerry struggled to remember what he was doing three days before, and almost dreamily told Newman that "I killed the whole day Friday."

The detective knew enough about Freudian slips to remember that one. Jerry insisted that he got to Chappell, Nebraska, late Friday night after riding all day and stayed overnight in a rest stop outside that little town in the western panhandle, and left there Saturday morning, driving a couple of exits east to get gas, then turning back west for home by mid-morning Saturday. So he never rode even close to Iowa.

Newman listened to the tape of his interview later on Sunday and noticed that Jerry seemed to jump into a stuttering mode, rambling, repeating, sounding far more nervous than a guy who was just explaining a joyride to find himself. He played this particular section of the tape twice, listening as Jerry explained his sleepover in Nebraska:

Mark: "Oh, uh, I think it's Chappell or something like this…"

Newman: "Nebraska?"

M: "Nebraska—it's out in the western panhandle."

N: "And that was on Interstate 80 also?"

Mark: "That was a regular—Nebraska rest area with improved shelters and heated restrooms, you know, and I shaved and stuff, you know, I could clean up there."

N: "Uh huh."

Mark: "There was a sign saying not to camp there, but I did camp there anyway. Nice place."

And so it went. Newman had to admit, Jerry's politeness and ready smile could probably charm the devil out of an air conditioner. He was one polite fellow.

The interview finished, they shook hands, and Newman thanked them for their time. He immediately called Dutton's office and reported. Dutton planned on having both Jerry and Mimi interviewed as soon as possible after the funeral. No way was he going to let either of them get back to California without more questions.

14: Leslie Mark Family Funeral

THE FUNERAL, HELD Tuesday at the Cedar Falls Trinity United Methodist Church, overflowed with mourners. Reporters from local and state papers estimated attendance at eight hundred people from Iowa and beyond, many of them profoundly grief-stricken. Everyone remembered something good about the young Marks—how they loved their children, how much they volunteered for local groups, how Les seemed to have a good sense of himself in the community. Les had endeared himself for his generosity, and people remarked on how much they would miss his willingness to donate time, energy, and money to all sorts of charitable causes.

Four caskets—two adult and two child-sized—were positioned at the front of the church, unopened, their covers facing the altar. The funeral home director worried that a hysterical mourner might actually run up to the caskets and try to open one, so he purposely had the caskets turned around and sealed.

Investigators, who often attended funerals of victims, felt no surprise at the overflow of mourners, nor that many of them were unable to contain their grief. The church echoed with soft weeping and sobs. No small talk or friendly chatter. Friends and neighbors of the Marks felt numbed by what seemed like an intrusion of unbridled evil, a dark force they could hardly imagine. When they talked at all, they talked around rather than about the murders. "We're all going to miss them." "I can't believe we won't see them again." "Why, I just saw them last week at the Eagle store."

Eldest brother Richard doubled as minister and pallbearer, and his eulogy, delivered in ministerial tones, spoke of what wonderful people the community had lost, "the kind of people who come along once in a generation," as he put it. He suggested that the person who most needed their prayers was the murderer, and that mourners should pray to God that He be merciful to "them or him."

The service lasted barely forty-five minutes, with only congregational singing, Richard's eulogy, and a consoling message from Rev. Burris, the family minister. Burris had recently begun his pastorship at their church and wasn't as close to the family as Don Iles, the previous long-time pastor, so his message about grief and consolation didn't resonate with mourners as did Richard's heartfelt message. Citizens of the Cedar Valley knew that this crime would get woven deeply into the warp and weft of local history, the darkest of threads.

Jerry left the church behind the caskets with Mimi on his arm, head bowed in grief, following his father, mother, and Tom. Behind them came Jorjean's parents George and Margaret Colthurst, looking grim and bereft. Richard was among the first out of the church, helping carry Les's casket.

Investigators noticed that Jerry appeared deeply disturbed, even crushed. He wiped away tears several times and seemed to cling to his mother when they had arrived. She literally held him up at times, like a hospital attendant. Tom appeared his usual lost self, unable to connect. Dorothy was a tough woman who didn't betray emotion, nor did her husband Wayne, plainly suffering his own hell. Both looked beaten and bowed, though not defeated. Midwesterners through and through, they reflected taciturnity and acceptance, though obviously shaken and numb.

A contingent from the funeral drove with headlights on past the homeplace on Mark Road to nearby Gerholdt Cemetery where four graves had been readied. They gathered as Reverend Burris read the "ashes to ashes" message. The homeplace sat less than a mile to the southeast, not visible from the tiny cemetery. Dorothy had wanted them to be buried in a cemetery in Cedar Falls, but the Colthursts insisted that Jorjean would have preferred burial near her beloved farm. Dorothy did not get her way this time.

15: Investigating Continues

AFTER THE FUNERAL BCI agents returned to their Black Hawk County Courthouse war room. They felt focused, energized by the sheer weight and horror of the crime. By Wednesday, they had turned their full attention to Jerry Mark and his whereabouts during the murders. Some twenty investigators had taken a recent photo of Jerry and were talking with employees at gas stations, restaurants, and rest stops along several two-lane roads down to Interstate 80 then on I-80 itself all the way to the Pacific coast. Most of them worked the case because they wanted it solved. They were hunting a child-killer, a monster.

They had been briefed on Jerry's interview in South Lake Tahoe, and knowing the range of the Honda, gave special attention to gas stations that sat every 120-140 miles from where they first positively ID'd him filling up. They worked all sites where workers or tourists might have observed a lone motorcyclist. It was tedious work, but there were no shortcuts.

Meanwhile, Dutton and Ruxlow prepared investigators for more interviews. Dorothy and Wayne were brought in, as well the Colthursts, and Clark and Carol Renner, Victor Mark, and Dennis and Barbara Wulf. They scheduled Mimi for Friday morning and Jerry for that afternoon, and brought in a polygraph specialist from Des Moines. Dutton kept hoping for some hard evidence that would exonerate Jerry, but nothing came.

Reports arrived from the field both Wednesday and Thursday. An investigator called from Berkeley saying that Mimi had phoned her father on Saturday after the murders telling him the gun that she and Jerry had taken from her husband's camper was missing from their storage shed, along with an Iowa plate from Jerry's smaller motorcycle. But Newman's report from his Monday interview showed that by then Mimi wasn't exactly sure whether the gun was missing, and that Jerry and Mimi felt they had to return to Berkeley to verify its whereabouts before they flew back for the funeral. Evidently she hadn't searched the contents of the storage locker thoroughly after it had been burglarized.

Then there was Lesley Warren, the rest stop attendant in Chappell, Nebraska. Investigators talked to him on Thursday and he said that yes, he had seen a motorcyclist matching Jerry's description—but on Friday, October 31, not Saturday morning. That meant Jerry could make Northeast Iowa from Nebraska by late Friday evening. Dutton's office then received a letter that Jerry had written Les (Bill Sindlinger, the Mark family lawyer, brought it in, having received it from the police after the post office delivered it to the homeplace) dated October 27 in which Jerry asked Les to falsify his employment record. Jerry wrote:

"What I would appreciate being able to do, is to list in the 'previous employment' section of future job applications that I farmed with you as a general partner during the 1973 and 1974 crop years, or from March of 1973 to December of 1974..."

Les never received the letter, and it gave Jerry reason to insist that he and Les were mending fences. To Dutton, the letter revealed Jerry's willingness to shade the truth for his own benefit.

16: Questioning Mimi

THAT FRIDAY MORNING, less than a week after the murders, interviewers focused on Mimi first. They put her at ease with assurances that she could help find the real killer. "We're sure you want to find whoever did this just as much as we do. That's why we're interviewing family members." She admitted that made sense.

Her answers corroborated what Jerry had told detective Newman, which wasn't surprising, since she had heard Jerry's story several times by then. She remembered receiving calls from Coalinga and Provo, which would have made a trip to Iowa impossible, given time frames for the ride and the murders.

Toward the end of the interview, though, she admitted she had some trouble with Jerry's story at first. "I was suspicious, you know, all these things happened, that license plate was gone, I started thinking wild thoughts and so I went to check the license plate, you know—how you get freaky and weird?"

The investigator helped her with that thought.

"Well, I don't think it's weird if you have a missing license plate and gun, and a trip where you can't contact someone who had access to both."

Mimi paused at that, realizing how Jerry's trip and the storage shed burglary must look. Jerry had succeeded in helping her overcome doubts with steady reassurances. "Mimi, you can't believe I could kill anyone, really..." And she couldn't, nor could Rebecca, his ex-wife. Nor could anyone, really. It was just too awful.

To the question, "Has Jerry told you anything that would strike you as funny?" She replied, "No, and I can honestly say no because," and she hesitated, realizing that she was about to disclose an intimate fact, but thought it would help them understand. Continuing, "OK, sexually if Jerry's frustrated—upset, nervous, you know he can't—he can't do anything, you know what I mean—and he's fine that way now—he's sleeping well too. Things like that are evidence to me that this investigation today doesn't bother him at all. A guilty guy wouldn't act that way."

Both investigators felt taken aback, and she continued, "I was very upset at my father for calling the police without asking me about the gun—connecting it right up to the crime. I thought he had no business calling the police. But when I told Jerry he said he thought my dad should have called the police, you know, if the gun's missing... "

Mimi's interview ended with her certainty that Jerry would agree to a polygraph. "He'll do all this stuff because he knows he didn't do it." They told their polygraph expert to prepare tests for both Mimi and Jerry.

17: Questioning Jerry

JERRY'S INTERVIEW STARTED while Mimi was taking a lie detector test. The same two investigators interrogated him. They knew Mimi had been suspicious of Jerry, and that Alga's stolen revolver fired the same odd caliber bullets the forensics detectives had taken from the murder scene. All were aware that Jerry didn't contact her after Thursday night until Sunday.

Jerry, nervous but assured, responded without hesitation to early questions about his post-high school life, offering detailed information on his Peace Corps stint, his months in Naval Officer Candidate School, his subsequent refusal of an officer's commission, his return to Iowa during the summer of '69 to farm, his going to law school, his passing the Iowa Bar Exam, his attempts to work as a political operative for Iowa congressional candidates, his recent move to California, and his current search for employment. To him, he was giving facts, and stayed true to them. To his questioners he was reciting a steady decline, a drift into aimlessness.

He explained his motorcycle trip, with the locations—Coalinga, Barstow, Vegas, Provo, calling Mimi from Coalinga and Provo on Wednesday and Thursday nights, then riding to the rest stop near Chappell, staying there on the night of the murders and starting back to Berkeley from western Nebraska Saturday. Then he hitched a ride from Cheyenne to just outside Salt Lake City from Larry Rauch in his truck, pulling a horse trailer with his motorcycle aboard. Sunday afternoon he called Evelyn Callenberg, Mimi's mother, at her home in South Lake Tahoe, California person to person collect, asking for Mimi. Evelyn told him to "call home," but he thought she meant Berkeley, not Iowa. Investigators had been briefed on this story, but needed to hear Jerry's version.

Jerry explained that when he called Mrs. Callenberg again a few minutes later and actually talked to her, she broke the awful news. Shocked and grief-stricken, he managed to ride to Carson City, Nevada, where he met Mimi and her father. He followed them on the Honda to South Lake Tahoe. The next day he and Mimi drove to Berkeley, then flew to Waterloo for the funeral.

Then the two skeptical detectives pressed him. "OK, Jerry, we want to give you a polygraph test. Your brother Richard took one, and Mimi's doing one now. This will clear up any suspicions."

Jerry looked dumbstruck. "Well, I just don't know about this. Can you give me a few minutes to think about it?"

Not a problem, they said, and asked when they returned, "Well, what's your verdict Jerry, what do you think?"

"Well, it just gets my back up a little bit too much—"

"That we asked you?"

"Yeah—and I hope you'll understand and I just don't want to do that—but I'm going to talk to Mom about it and see."

"You don't wish to take the polygraph?"

"Not at this time."

"What is your hesitation, if we might ask?"

"Well I just…," Jerry went completely blank. He had no idea how to refuse their request without seeming guilty.

They pressed. "If you feel slighted because you were asked, like we said before, we've asked all your relatives."

"No, that's not it, I just—"

"In other words, then, you're up tight about it?"

"Well, I'm Les's brother, you know, and to be asked to take a lie detector test related to his murder just rubs me the wrong way. I want to discuss it with Mom and Dad before I give permission."

"So it rubs you the wrong way to be asked?"

"Yes sir." Jerry went into his polite mode.

Both investigators felt they had little to lose by cornering him. The stakes were too high not to try. Dutton felt that the odd-cartridge missing revolver tipped suspicions into probabilities, so he had told them to push. If Jerry invoked his right to remain silent, well, that was that. In the process they might get him to confess, or at least give away more than he knew.

"You tried, Jerry, you almost had it made. We were looking at other people before you, but things just fell into place—things just clicked— the missing .38 caliber shells, a rare shell that we're looking for, the license plate, the trip, the deaths that weekend, the inconsistencies, the calls, the lack of calls, the lack of concern at various spots, two and two are not five, we know it, Jerry. Things just don't add up."

Then: "Why the kids? The kids tear us up—all of us personally—we usually don't get this personally involved in a case—we've all got kids— that tore us up—and the first thing we ask is why and that's what I'm asking you—why those kids?"

Jerry felt cornered and sick. Panic welled up, but he wasn't about to give in to bullying. The bastards, he thought.

"Things are closing in, Jerry, you can feel the pressure—you've felt it here—we've hit sensitive points and you light up like a thermometer— the clock has stopped—you tell us, Jerry, you tell us why—"

Jerry was stunned with their directness, and determined to invoke his right to remain silent. He could only mumble, "Oh, God, this is… a…I don't know… .I don't know what makes you do this to me—"

"That's not the question—what made you do that to the family?"

"I didn't do that... " Then he went silent. He had had enough. He knew what they were doing, and asked to leave. They had no legal right to detain him. They shook their heads as he left the interrogation room, sure he had been lying, but unable to prove it.

Trembling, Jerry wrote Mimi a note as he was leaving and gave it to one of the detectives to pass on to Mimi. "Mimi, I love you. I have been accused of killing Les, Jorjean, and the kids. But I'm not under arrest. I did not do it. I want to see you, and I am at home with the folks. Love, Jerry." The detectives confiscated the note.

18: Failed Polygraph

MIMI'S LIE DETECTOR test, which she had finished during Jerry's interview, had in fact yielded useful information. The interviewer determined that she had probably not been truthful on several questions, according to her stress levels, as he filed in his report on November 12th.

The polygraph examiner asked: "Do you suspect Jerry of shooting the Mark family?"

"No, not at all."

"Do you know for sure if Jerry shot any of the Mark family?"

"I'm absolutely sure he couldn't have."

"Before Jerry left, did you know he was going to Iowa?"

"I didn't know one way or another, but believed him when he said he was riding south, not east."

"When Jerry returned from his trip did he tell you he had been in Iowa?"

"He never got that far. I believe him."

"When Jerry left do you know for sure if he had a gun?"

Mimi hesitated. "I know for sure that he didn't." But she shifted in the chair and blinked several times, and her stress levels spiked.

"Did Jerry tell you where he threw his sweatshirt away?" Jerry had mentioned his sweatshirt to Detective Newman during the first interview. Now they needed it because it might contain evidence—blood or microscopic particles. Investigators were searching along I-80 in Wyoming and Utah, but knew that was a kernel in a silo.

"No, he didn't mention it, and I doubt he would remember. He was exhausted, you know."

Mimi's answers and her stress levels didn't add up. Afterward the examiner wrote, "the subject was not telling the complete truth at the time of the examination."

Dutton had told the polygraph expert to call him immediately after he had calculated the results, and gave instructions to keep Mimi and Jerry around until he heard the examiner's report. The examiner also mentioned that Mimi had worried that Jerry might be involved in the murders, and that even Rebecca had worried about him based on the timing of his trip and the missing revolver.

Dutton heard the report, compared this information with what he knew from both that day's interview—Jerry's refusal to take a polygraph, and in his November 3rd interview with Newman. Jerry had stuck to his story, and was waiting for Mimi to finish so they could return to his folk's house.

Dutton faced a dilemma. Mimi seemed to be covering up. She either knew something or thought she knew something but felt afraid to talk. Jerry, on the other hand, had shut down, no longer the polite, cooperative citizen. Invoking his right to silence virtually guaranteed they had to let him go.

To arrest Jerry, Dutton needed more than coincidences and a motorcycle ride. Yet he was their only real suspect, and Mimi might be their best shot until more evidence emerged. He decided to have her arrested.

This strategy meant a possible false arrest suit, but he felt justified. Dutton would hold her for a few days, hoping she would crack, or at least inadvertently provide real evidence. That would keep Jerry around too. If Jerry fled the state while Mimi was in jail, that would point to his guilt as well. It was a win-win decision, though not for Mimi.

Mimi's arrest floored Jerry, who considered it blatant harassment. But for now, there was nothing he could do, and Dutton sought to make sure Mimi knew that withholding information about a felony made her subject to imprisonment.

With Mimi in jail, Jerry stayed home with his parents, and all of them fumed and fussed. Jerry felt betrayed and miserable, but managed to remain confident and upbeat when he spoke to his parents. He assured them that cops are always desperate to arrest someone and would leap to conclusions based on nothing more than coincidences.

The elder Marks fully supported Jerry, as did the Reverends Burris and Iles, as well as friends who remembered him as the all-American kid. As he told them, he was being victimized by sloppy detective work. He stayed angry and indignant, as did his mother and her friends.

19: Arrest

JERRY NOW BELIEVED his own arrest was imminent. He had kept Mimi in the dark, and she still trusted him. He was well aware that she knew plenty that would look bad under cross-examination. Nothing more. After all, she was his buffer, his all-around supporter, at least as good as his mom. Dorothy and Mimi together formed a formidable team, and that comforted him. But it probably wasn't enough to keep him from getting arrested. Damn that Dutton and his henchmen, he repeated to anyone who would listen.

He knew Mimi feared his roiling temper, as had Rebecca. They found him incorrigibly controlling, and Mimi had often wondered why he couldn't find and keep a decent job. They lived low on the hog in a state where there was plenty of work for minimum wage at least, and much better for anyone with education and ambition.

Jerry had plenty of education but little ambition. For a time, he tried to channel his anger. Instead of whining and making an ass of himself, he took action. But now he struggled. Arresting Mimi! With nothing but a polygraph for evidence! He knew Dutton was grasping at straws, playing the intimidation card. Yet he felt surprised by how fast they were moving, how determined they seemed. This was dangerous, since cops on a mission with the power of the state behind them could do anything. Wrongful convictions were surprisingly common. He began to think about hiring a lawyer. He might need someone who could handle Dutton, and it probably wasn't Sindlinger.

He planned to explain to his folks why Mimi was in jail and develop a convincing story about why they suspected him. That night when he walked into the living room, Dorothy and Wayne were sitting on their couch looking forlorn and frightened. His father had seemed utterly destroyed by the week's events, and now this. His mom wouldn't look at him. "Mom, Dad—you're not going to believe why the goddamn bastards have arrested Mimi."

"Jerry, you know I don't appreciate cussing. Well, what happened? Tell us." Dorothy glowered at both her husband and son. None of them had been sleeping well, and their faces showed heavy fatigue in deepening lines and dark circles.

"Well, they think Mimi knows something. I guess she had trouble with that stupid lie detector test. We studied polygraphs in law school and they're completely unreliable. Cops only use them when they don't have evidence."

Jerry's mother sat bolt upright, expressing her alarm. "What have they charged her with?"

"I'm not sure, but they must think she knows something and is keeping it from them."

His father looked stricken. "Jerry, what in hell is going on?"

"Dad, you know what's going on. They're desperate to pin it on someone. They have to make an arrest, and I'm their only suspect. Why, I don't know, but they're twisting Mimi's words to get her to tell them what they need to hear. Anyone can flunk or pass a lie detector test depending on how well they lie."

This was in fact true, but Jerry knew his dad might not buy it. Wayne Mark was an old-time law and order man, had always believed in police rectitude and professionalism. An arrest meant guilt.

Jerry pressed on. "Dad, you wouldn't believe what I've seen in California. The cops arrest anyone and pin crimes on them. Nobody trusts them. They're lazy as hell and don't bother real criminals." His dad looked skeptical, but nodded. It was all too much.

Dorothy wanted more. "Jerry, I don't believe that Dutton would do that unless they had some evidence. Can't they be sued for false arrest?"

"They sure as hell can, and we'll do that. Meanwhile, we ought to get her out on bond. What do you say to that?"

"How much? We might be able to put up a little, but we can't do it now, on Friday night, can we?" His mother was going to be harder to lean on than his dad, at least about Mimi's bail. No surprise there.

"Yeah we can't do much until Monday morning. Damn them any-way. And it's going to be real money, since it's a murder charge. Not sure how much we'll need." Jerry felt reluctant to pressure them on Mimi's behalf, since they barely knew her. He wasn't even positive she would marry him, though he sure as hell was going to try. He knew Mimi could sink him.

"Jerry, I'm worried," his mother stared at him. She was trembling, looking as though she might break down. "We can't defend her and you both, and I still don't understand this arrest. What did she tell them? Where was she when Les was murdered? Surely they don't sus-pect her?"

"No, no, and Mom, they don't even really suspect me. They know better. They just have to show results. The entire Midwest is terrified. They're the worst killings anyone can remember. God, who would shoot little kids? The cops take this personally, and they're out for blood. They go for the nearest suspects, and we're it, believe it or not. God Damn It anyway!" Jerry was on fire.

His mother flinched. "So they're jumping on a bandwagon? Jerry, what did you do that makes them even care about you? Where WERE you when Les was murdered?" She needed a real answer.

"Mom, you know my story, and it's the truth. I know it looks bad, me being out there in Nebraska and not seeing Renato. I was in a hurry to get back to Mimi and didn't want to bother. Besides, I wasn't into socializing. I was just riding to think about my future and all, you know? I've told you before. You have to believe me."

He looked at his mother imploringly, knowing she had little choice. What mother could ever believe that one of her sons would deliberately murder the other?

"Well, I believe you, but how will we convince them? They don't know you. You've got to have evidence. Weren't there some eyewit-nesses on Friday or Saturday?"

"Yes, and I've told them. They're still looking. And—oh god." He bowed his head and clenched his jaw.

"What is it?" his father asked.

"Jesus Christ, this is terrible."

"Now what?" Dorothy seemed ready to explode.

"Shit, I just remembered. You know how I like to write, that I took some journalism classes. Last month I was thinking about writing an article about the Symbionese Liberation Army. You know they live right near us in Berkeley. I thought I could get in good with them if I gave them something, you know, to prove myself."

"Jerry, what are you saying? You didn't buy a gun, did you?" Now she was angry.

"No, but I did buy some bullets. Not far from Rebecca's. I thought if I gave these radicals a box of cartridges they might believe I could be trusted."

They both looked at him like he had just round-housed them. Stricken. Undone.

"Why, Jerry, we're dead. They've got you. Were they the same type of bullets that killed Les and Jorjean?"

"Shit, Mom, I don't know. They could be. I didn't pay much attention, just bought what seemed to be bullets these radicals could use."

His father spoke up, loudly. "God DAMN, Jerry. How could you be so stupid? Do you know how this looks? They've got you." He went into a rant. "You know this won't look like a coincidence. This looks like you set out to kill your own brother. They're going to use that against you every step of the way. How in hell are we going to fight that?"

His mother chimed in. "Jerry, you're too smart for your own good. What do you care about the Symbionese Liberation Army? Why would you ever want to write anything about them? You're crazy, you know that?"

Jerry grew defensive. "I know it, I know it. But one coincidence doesn't make me a murderer. We'll prove I wasn't there. I know we

93

can do that. We need to set up a reward for anyone who helps find the murderer. Can we do that?"

"Yes, of course," his mother said. "But Jerry, you've put us in an awful position. We look like fools. They're going to have evidence and all we have is your word."

"I know, Mom, I know. But we'll get through it. In five years we'll laugh at this."

"Jerry," his dad's gaunt face took on the darkest scowl Jerry had ever seen. "We will never laugh at this." And that ended it.

Jerry went to the guest bedroom and tried to call Mimi. The county jail operator said she was not available, and he flopped on the bed, miserable. Exhausted from his own mental torments, he dozed.

In a barren, hazy landscape, he felt pursued. Run! Run! He found himself dashing along on a road that ran into woods, then out into a shopping mall parking lot, then along a creek. Something was behind him, a force that he couldn't see or identify. No matter how he twisted and turned, feinted and ducked, it homed in on him, seemed to swoop at him, like blackbirds protecting their young.

The more he ran, the hotter he grew, until he felt drenched in sweat. Even his wet skin didn't cool him, and he couldn't catch his breath. He was panting like a dog. He wanted to lash out, scream at whatever was making him run, but whenever he looked back, there was just a void. He kept running, getting more heated, more exhausted.

He stirred awake, forced himself to calm down. They had nothing, he knew. Nothing beyond circumstances that looked bad. He had a real alibi, and knew he could outsmart them. They wouldn't believe him capable of murder, least of all a heinous slaughter of children. And would they find anything in California coming from Iowa? That was his insurance. Rubes on the road.

Meanwhile, Dutton and Ruxlow took calls from investigators around the country, hoping they would get something that would help make a case for Jerry's arrest. Interviewers kept grilling Mimi, but she decided on Saturday that she wouldn't talk without a lawyer, so they gave up, though still hoping she might change her mind. Sindlinger convinced her that talking any more to the police was worse than useless.

Frustrated, investigators turned to emerging evidence. On November 9th they got their break. After BCI agents heard from their field investigators in California, they called Dutton's office. The agents had been tracing Jerry's travels around Berkeley and points south when he visited his daughters. Seems he rode his newly acquired Honda down the coast to visit his soon-to-be ex-wife Rebecca and daughters. As Rebecca had told them, Jerry had shown them the new motorcycle, and his daughters helped cut his hair and beard. Rebecca described this endearing father-daughter bonding memory, and remarked on how happy Jerry had seemed, that he was looking forward to a motorcycle ride sometime in late October, and wanted to spend time with his daughters before he took off.

BCI investigators traced that very route down the California coast, stopping at all gun shops and sporting goods stores who stock cartridges, in particular those .38 Long Colt variety.

Just a block off Highway 101 in Paso Robles, they pulled in to Ken's Sporting Goods. The amiable clerk was happy to help, and though he couldn't identify Jerry from the photo they had shown him, he did remember selling a box of .38 Long Colt cartridges.

Jack Makendonsky looked at the store's record book in which he recorded names, social security numbers, the purchased ammo, and the date. After a short search, he found it. "Ah, there it is—the guy signed for it and gave his social security number." He turned the book around and the investigators stared at the signature, both signed and printed: Jerry Mark, along with his social security number.

"You know, I do sort of remember a conversation with him. He showed me his Iowa driver's license, and I mentioned that I was from

Iowa too—Waterloo, where you're from. We talked about being from Iowa." The detectives could hardly believe their luck. Eight days after the murders, they knew about the weapon, and here they had a legal record of the victim's brother buying those virtually obsolete cartridges. They bought the dealer's remaining two boxes for the labs.

This all happened on Saturday, so a warrant would have to be sworn out, and they could arrest him on Monday, and get him arraigned and possibly behind bars almost immediately. Unless the world's most bizarre coincidence just occurred, they had their murderer. Proving it to a jury was another matter, but this a solid start.

On Monday, Jerry, who had reached Mimi a couple of times on the phone but hadn't visited her, was in fact expecting a police car. He told his parents that the local cops were probably going to arrest him, and they shouldn't try to prevent them or say anything. They didn't know how to reply, so they kept quiet, looking defeated. Jerry decided to go outside and poke around in his mom's flower bed to occupy himself, knowing they could come any time. The squad car arrived after 3:00, and two sheriff's deputies strode to him as he was weeding the peony bed. Jerry noticed that Bill Sindlinger pulled up behind the deputies' car just as they spoke.

"Jerry Mark, we have warrants for your arrest for the murders of Les, Jorjean, Julie, and Jeffrey Mark."

Jerry nodded, not knowing how else to respond.

"You have the right to remain silent…" they read him his full Miranda rights, then asked "Do you understand your rights at this time?"

"Yes, I do," Jerry said almost under his breath and looked back at the house. He could see his mother and father looking out at them.

"You will have to come with us to be arraigned and plead," said the detective, and they cuffed him and led him to the squad car. Dutton had arranged for a judge to stand by, with a preliminary hearing still that afternoon.

Dutton felt elated—and deeply troubled.

20: Jerry and Mimi

JERRY SPENT A TERRIBLE first night in the county jail, struggling to believe what was happening and raging at the legal machinery that had him cornered. He wasn't sure what they had discovered, but couldn't believe they had found anything that put him at the homeplace the night of the murders. He had made no mistakes, left no prints and no one had seen him coming or going. In fact, they only had that rumor about the brothers and father fighting over the will. Nothing, really.

He wondered whether they had discovered he had bought ammunition out in Paso Robles. He was glad he broke that news to his parents already. If so, the bastards were smarter than he thought, or at least more dogged.

He lay on his cot and dozed, hating the idea of jail time. They had no business arresting him. Goddamn them anyway, he mumbled several times, and felt terrible about his poor folks having to see their son carted off in a squad car. He would get the hell out tomorrow and never come back. They couldn't hold him without more evidence than they had, and his folks would pay to get him out. They would have no problem hiring the best lawyer in the state to nail that smartass Dutton. Too eager to prove his brilliance, too willing to jump to conclusions and arrest the first suspect. He worked himself into righteous indignation, and maintained that stance from then on.

As he drifted off, more dreams arose. These were more fragmented, less predictable, almost abstract. One image kept arising, threading through the others like a motif: Ice. It floated at times all around him, sometimes encased him, other times pelted him like sleet, even hailed down on him from above. Almost every dream that night seemed to connect with winter: cold, ice, freezing.

Tuesday morning he woke to hear from the deputy that his mother was there, wanting to see him. He needed to keep reassuring her that he was all right, that this was going to go away. He was concerned about Mimi, too. She must be held in the same building, probably frantic and depressed. He ate the county jail breakfast—cold scrambled eggs, orange juice and coffee, and waited until he could go to the visitors' room.

He found Dorothy waiting for him over a small partition, looking pale and distraught. She was more concerned about Jerry than herself.

"Jerry, you look terrible. Didn't you sleep? Your dad and I stayed up most of the night. What should we do? I don't know anything about this criminal system... " She seemed disoriented.

"Mom, just relax. This is all a terrible mistake. We'll sort it out. Take a few deep breaths." Dorothy nodded, and literally drew a few breaths before speaking.

"Really, I know they're rushing this and had no business arresting you, but it feels terrible seeing you in jail." She wanted to shout at him, but held back. Never could she have imagined this nightmare.

"Yes, and I'll never forgive them for this. What's happened to Mimi? Have you talked to her?"

"We talked to her last night and told her about your being arrested. She wasn't surprised. They're going to let her out tomorrow, she thought. But what about you? What can we do?" Dorothy needed answers, desperately wanting to make this go away.

"I've thought about this. We have to move fast. First, hire the best lawyer in Iowa. These cops are determined, and we'll have to find someone who's more determined than they are."

"OK, Jerry, we'll do that right away. Who?"

"Lawrence Scalise. He was Iowa Attorney General in the mid-sixties and works out of Des Moines. He's our best chance."

"Jerry, he's going to be expensive. Why do we need such a good lawyer? You're innocent!"

"Yes, Mom, but this is the law. We have to be able to prove it, and the prosecution will make a big deal out of those coincidences. Scalise will tear them apart, so he'll be worth it."

"All right. I'll talk to your dad. Then what?"

"Get me out of here. I'm no jailbird. We'll post bond before a judge so I can go free until the trial. Get Sindlinger on this today, Mom, and set a court date. See how much they need and pay it. I need to help find the killer, and I can't do it in here."

Bill Sindlinger had helped his dad with all his real estate dealings, and served as family advisor on legal matters. He could handle getting Jerry out on bond, no trouble. Especially since they all knew Jerry posed no flight risk, and eventually would be exonerated. Besides, Dorothy Mark wasn't about to let her son rot in jail. Not while they could afford bail.

By late Tuesday, Sindlinger managed to get a bond hearing the next day, so Jerry would stay just one more night in jail. Meanwhile, the Marks learned that bond was to be set at a million dollars—which didn't surprise anyone. They also learned that the judge would accept just twenty percent in cash for bail after Jerry appeared with Bill Sindlinger and agreed to terms.

Jerry was released on Wednesday on $200,00 dollars bond. He was free to come and go, and the Marks would forfeit that amount should Jerry break his agreement to follow the terms. He was to freely submit to any tests ordered by the prosecutor, he was not allowed to leave the state, and he was to stay with his parents until trial, probably in the spring.

Jerry agreed to those conditions, and thanked his stars for his parents. He felt more determined than ever to prove his innocence now that his freedom was assured. Feeling vindicated, innocent until trial, then permanently free, he began to see his future as assured and rosy. After all, wealthy people almost never go to prison.

Now to go to work on his case. He would meet with Scalise later that week, but right now he needed to sooth Mimi. She was released with him, and they left the county courthouse with his parents to drive back home.

None of them spoke. Mimi looked pale and drained. Though Jerry felt optimistic, she didn't share his upbeat attitude, so he kept it to himself. Wayne retired to the bedroom, and Dorothy retreated into the kitchen to make coffee.

Jerry and Mimi sat together at the dining room table, finally alone and able to talk, and Jerry didn't mind if his mom overheard. After all, both women would have to testify for him at trial, so they might as well hear his story again. Mimi trembled as she spoke. "Jerry, it was awful. They didn't believe anything I said after I failed that lie detector. County jail was just hell. Terrible food, no privacy, nasty facilities. I never want to go though that again." She struggled to hold back tears.

"Don't worry, you won't have to. So sorry they arrested you. I've got Bill looking into a false arrest charge. We'll sue the bastards. They can't just willy-nilly arrest people."

"They thought they had you, and me, and that we might have planned those awful murders. I can't believe they would get that desperate."

"You know they have to arrest someone fast or their asses are grass. They're terrified of looking incompetent, so they jump on the nearest suspect. Why they suspect me still eludes me." Jerry wanted to sound indignant.

Then Mimi unloaded. "DAMN you Jerry! You know how terrible it looks. You leave our place Wednesday morning on a big motorcycle, you stay in touch Wednesday and Thursday, then I don't talk to you until Sunday. They're murdered early Saturday morning. And Alga's gun gets stolen the morning you leave, along with your license plate. Then my own dad calls the cops. From their point of view, you really do look suspicious. Shit, Jerry, if I were them I'd arrest you too. And probably me as well. What the hell…" she trailed off, covered her face and began sobbing.

They had scared her half to death. Jerry realized he needed her, badly.

"OK, Mimi, OK. I really do understand. It's all right. I love you so much. You've been nothing but wonderful through this. We have to stick together. I guess I might as well ask right now: Will you marry me?"

She stopped sobbing and looked at him in disbelief.

"What? Jerry, you want me to marry you now?"

"I do, and I mean it from the bottom of my heart. I didn't know I could love someone so much. I think we should spend the rest of our lives together. I can't imagine happiness with anyone else." He looked at her longingly, beseechingly. Even with no makeup and a tear-streaked face she looked perfect, a soulmate. He really did love her, or so he thought as he gazed into her eyes. She was a beautiful woman, and still on his side.

She paused and stared for what seemed like minutes.

"Jerry, I don't know what to say. I'm not even sure they'll let us get married. They probably want to call me as a witness for the prosecution. But yes, I guess if they will let us, I will marry you. I love you too,

Jerry. You couldn't kill anyone. But they're making a case, and you're going to need all the help you can get."

"That's wonderful, Mimi. We'll make my defense together, then you and I can move back to Iowa to take care of Mom and Tom and Dad."

Mimi looked horrified for a moment at this prospect. "Well, we'll see, Jerry. I'm not at all sure that's a good idea. I still don't think you know what you're up against. They're getting more evidence by the day, and here you're going to be sitting around in your folks' place."

"Well, Mom and Dad have agreed to put up a $10,000 reward to find the murderer, and I can nose around all I want. I'll get a job and keep investigating. I'll find the killers so we can get out of here. That's going to be my purpose in life. That, and marrying and loving you."

Mimi needed to hear this, and she hugged him. "Jerry, I want you to get your act together. Do exactly what you say you'll do, and don't stay around here working at some silly job. Work on the evidence. If you don't do that, they'll nail you, and I mean it." As if adding an afterthought, she said, "Yes, I'll marry you, Jerry."

They embraced and held each other for a few moments with Jerry looking soulfully into her eyes. He wondered if she had agreed to marry him more out of fear than love, but set that thought aside.

Finally they got up to tell Dorothy their news. She supported them completely, taking it as rare good news for Jerry.

21. Prosecution

DUTTON AND RUXLOW met several days a week starting in November. They talked strategy, planned testimony, anticipated defense tactics, and coordinated the search for more evidence and witnesses. Though they felt confident they had the right man, proving it was another matter. Juries had the final say, after all.

Lawrence Scalise and his partner, John Sandre, were known as thorough, meticulous lawyers. When Dutton heard that the Mark family had retained them as Jerry's defense counsel, he knew he needed to build an impeccable case. Scalise was a detail man, and would object to the slightest overreaching, speculating, opinionating—every step of the way. Plus Dorothy and Wayne seemed willing to spend whatever it took to free their innocent Jerry.

Then there was Jerry and Mimi. Dutton was hoping for a subpoena to put Mimi on the stand as a witness for the prosecution. She could offer information that would show Jerry planned his trip well in advance, that he had tried to get her out of Berkeley to stay with her brother for the entire week—implying serious premeditation—and that she had been downright frightened of him on Saturday and Sunday after the murders. She must have thought he was capable of murder until he persuaded her otherwise. What a gift for their case. Though they couldn't use her having failed the polygraph test as evidence, they could show that Mimi's immediate reactions to the murders involved suspicions. At the very least, that would embarrass the defense, who would portray Jerry as a victim of zealous investigators who stopped at nothing, and who had made serious errors while investigating.

Both men knew that Jerry would fear her testifying as much as they desired it. So he would manipulate her into a marriage, then invoke "spousal privilege," wherein a wife cannot be forced to testify against a husband. However, since the murders were committed before they were married, Dutton might make the case that she could in fact be forced to testify. Otherwise, as Mrs. Jerry Mark, Mimi Callenberg Forrest would be worse than useless, she would be unavailable. They began making plans to try to prevent a Mark-Forrest marriage, should it come to that.

They also knew that Scalise would try to keep the jury from hearing testimony or information in court that might prejudice them against a defendant—such as prior family squabbles or an injunction against a marriage—so any testimony along those lines in front of a jury would be challenged, and probably disallowed. They knew that would happen often during the trial and had to prepare for it.

A third struggle: evidence. So far they had found no hard evidence that placed Jerry at the crime scene. They had an expert examine the pliers they found in Jerry's Honda toolkit to see if that tool cut the telephone wires near the homeplace. No such luck. And they hoped for a good set of fingerprints from the crime scene. DNA testing, which Jerry used in later appeals, would not come into widespread use until the early 1990s.

The major boost in their case: those .38 Long Colt cartridges Jerry had purchased in Paso Robles, and signing his real name. Could he have been that dumb? Though Jack Makendonsky couldn't identify Jerry from photos or in a lineup as the purchaser, since he had given his signature and social security number, that didn't matter. Both Dutton and Ruxlow shook their heads as they discussed it, wondering how Jerry could have been so arrogant. And he lied about having ever purchased cartridges in his interview with Detective Newman. Did he think they wouldn't notice? Dutton planned to ask Jerry on the stand why he had lied about that in particular.

Ruxlow held a theory that as perpetrators travel further from the crime scene, they become more and more careless. On scene they're as careful as surgeons about what they touch and leave behind. A few miles away, they get sloppy. Two thousand miles away, they think they can do anything. Jerry must have figured that no thickheaded investigator would bother to trek all the way to Paso Robles and find that little sporting goods store. Jerry was not only gifted with a hot temper, he believed deeply in his own intelligence.

Now they were wondering what else they could find that would point to the same conclusion. Dutton thought about Jerry's phone calls to Mimi on Wednesday and Thursday nights. She had told both interviewers that she received calls from Jerry as he passed through Coalinga, near the Mojave Desert, then from Provo, Utah. But had the operator told her that, or had he paid for the calls himself and told her where he was? And did phone companies keep records of calls made to her number from wherever? He put a couple of investigators on it.

Then there was the Honda 450. BCI investigators had taken charge of Jerry's bike at Mimi's parents' place. They planned to dissect it bolt by bolt, looking for evidence of a disconnected odometer, a replaced or covered up California license plate or other evidence of unusual treatment and wear.

Finally, eyewitnesses. They needed to find people who could identify Jerry at various points, both from photos and in a line-up. The more the better. The key: times and dates. Jerry's alibi diverged markedly from what they had found, and Dutton wanted to poke as many holes in Jerry's story as he could.

That was their plan. Though they weren't especially happy about Jerry being out and about in the local community, they agreed that he wasn't a flight risk. They did wonder about Jerry's very public and constant insistence that he was being wrongly accused, and probably a change of venue for the trial was in order—not because Jerry couldn't get a fair trial in Black Hawk County, but because so many friends, relatives, and classmates believed in him. Dutton knew that Scalise would ask for a change of venue, and he wouldn't oppose it.

22. Defense

MEANWHILE, JERRY FELT desolate. He couldn't give way to despair, since that would make him useless for salvaging his future. He had to appear that he believed in his own innocence, absolutely and completely. For the most part, he succeeded.

His first test came when he actually met with Scalise and Sandre. They needed information, and Jerry, his mother, and Mimi met with them in Bill Sindlinger's office in Cedar Falls. Jerry needed Dorothy and Mimi with him at all times, and they were glad to oblige. Both had become thoroughly convinced he was being railroaded. The entire Mark family professed ongoing shock that Jerry was under arrest, and neither Scalise nor Sandre questioned him about actual guilt. All they wanted to know, as good lawyers would, was how easily they could refute the emerging evidence. To anyone who asked, they repeated that Jerry was being railroaded by a skilled prosecutor who was smart enough to have pieced together circumstantial evidence.

Innocent until proven guilty, they reminded everyone, and of course they were right. They knew they had a decent chance to get their client exonerated just on the sheer improbability of his murdering his own brother. Especially one who had been best man at his brother's wedding, and who had been a lawyer and now a peace-loving hippie, not long out of the Peace Corps.

Early on, Jerry raised his most pressing question: When could they get married? Scalise smiled. "Jerry, I can't imagine why you couldn't get married at any time, at least a few weeks after both of your divorces are final."

"Well, we do love each other and want to tie the knot as soon as possible. Would Dutton object, do you think?"

"Of course he'll object. He's bound to want to put her on the stand, thanks to her early statements and that failed polygraph. Keep in mind, Jerry, that we don't want it to look like you're scared of having her testify." Jerry professed his undying love, and that they were determined to marry. Dutton would just have to deal with it, and they couldn't imagine that a judge wouldn't rule in their favor.

With Mimi off the prosecution's table, they could concentrate on poking holes in eyewitnesses' testimony. But the bullets were another matter. "So you really did buy those .38 Long Colt cartridges, Jerry? What in god's name should we do about that? What did you do with them after you bought them?" Scalise knew that Dutton would ask these same questions eventually.

"I told you, and I'll say it to anyone. I wanted to get in tight with some SLA and Weathermen radicals around our neighborhood. I figured I could trade those bullets for an interview of some kind, and they would know they could trust me." He could see Mimi rolling her eyes ever so slightly at this. She desperately wanted to believe him, but this seemed like a stretch.

Scalise caught him up short, "Jerry, you didn't answer my question. What did you do with those cartridges? Can you produce the full box?"

Jerry shook his head. "Mr. Scalise, I did give them to some SLA guy in Berkeley, and he thanked me and never spoke to me again. They're long gone."

Scalise didn't press it. "OK, we can cross that bridge when we come to it. Now, Jerry, what else might those BCI guys discover? What about footprints at the scene? They claim they have some. And those bullets they found, they will try to match those with the slugs from the crime scene with the box they bought in Paso Robles. And eyewitnesses. We have to find people who saw you. That trucker in Cheyenne, for instance. We can use him. But they will try to use him, too."

Scalise narrowed his eyes as he looked at Jerry. The more Scalise described the evidence, the less certain he felt he could defend Jerry effectively. Dutton would make the most of every scrap, and Scalise would have to refute it from the beginning. He wasn't as confident as Jerry, who remained unshaken in his belief that they couldn't convict him without harder evidence. Nothing but coincidences, he reminded Scalise and Sandre over and over.

Jerry's phone calls from the road to their apartment's phone in Berkeley gave them all pause. The phone companies found records of every call and they weren't from where he had told investigators. Scalise knew they couldn't refute those, and shouldn't even try. Jerry couldn't believe they kept such exact records.

23. Trial I

SCALISE WANTED A change of venue. Negative publicity in the local media had made a fair trial impossible in Black Hawk County, he argued. The judge agreed, since coverage of the case occupied local and regional media for months, not to mention editorials and letters to the editor. The new trial venue became Sioux City, an Iowa meatpacking town sitting over 200 miles west of Cedar Falls/Waterloo. The old river city, founded in 1854 at the confluence of the Floyd and Missouri rivers, was also home to the ornate Woodbury County Courthouse, finished in 1918, a massive brick towered structure that had been put on the National Register of Historic Places for its "architectural uniqueness and sculptured details." It was an imposing building, and it now stood to house one of Iowa's most infamous murder cases. The All-American Boy as family murderer made the Mark trial downright mythical.

In the months before the trial Dutton and his team had lined up nearly 70 witnesses, all of whom were on notice to appear. Dutton had filed an injunction against Jerry and Mimi's "sham marriage," as he called it, insisting that a Mark/Forrest marriage would interfere with Mimi's obligation to serve as a witness for the prosecution. Dutton made the case before Judge Engelkes that their getting married would harm the cause of justice. The judge disagreed, saying they were free to get married, and several weeks before the trial the family held a small civil ceremony at Jerry's parents' home in Cedar Falls.

Jerry and Mimi ignored how it looked. Jerry hoped their marriage would damage the prosecution's case beyond repair. Without Mimi's testimony all evidence was purely circumstantial. Though Mimi knew nothing, she could be made to look like she had been played like a piano. Dutton would stop at nothing, he knew.

Surprisingly, as the trial drew nearer, Dutton stopped worrying about Mimi as a witness for the prosecution. Even without putting her on the stand, he had enough eyewitnesses placing Jerry in Iowa, and irrefutable evidence of Jerry's lies throughout his whole story.

The trial began in late May, 1976, with selection of jurors, which took nearly a week. Scalise and Sandre felt satisfied that they had gotten the best jury they could. They sought a panel of citizens who hadn't read or heard much about the case, and who held no particular prejudice against longhaired hippies or bikers. Dutton screened for jurors who wouldn't harbor doubts about Jerry's guilt due solely to his polite demeanor, advanced education, and tidy appearance, or for his lack of a criminal record.

Jerry, Scalise, and Sandre sat at the table in front of the judge, with friends of the Mark family in the first row behind them. Wayne stayed home, being too frail to make the trip. Dorothy and Mimi showed up at the courthouse every day, but did not attend the trial because either or both might give testimony. Potential witnesses were supposed to be sequestered from the trial, and they complied. The courtroom was always full, with friends, relatives, spectators, and print reporters (no cameras allowed) from all major Iowa papers and many from Nebraska and the Dakotas. George and Margaret Colthurst sat through the whole trial but avoided Mimi and Dorothy in the hallways and courthouse portico. They wanted nothing to do with their former in-laws.

From November to May, Dutton, Ruxlow, David Correll, and Harry Zanville plus some two dozen detectives and BCI agents had collaborated in preparing the prosecution's case. It grew into a mass of documents—thousands of pages—all of which the prosecution team had to pare down. Too much or marginal testimony would overwhelm or confuse a jury, and too little would help Scalise create reasonable doubt. Dutton sought balance.

Prosecutors were legally obliged to give the defense anything that might exonerate Jerry—"exculpatory evidence." Since "reasonable doubt" was the gold standard, Dutton felt pressure to offer every opportunity for the defense to make their strongest case. He didn't want to lose the case on appeal. He knew that Jerry Mark was perfectly capable of appealing for decades.

By the end of the first week, with the jury chosen and the usual list of jury instructions and requirements, the trial began. It was to last nearly a month, into June of 1976.

Dutton opened with an extended statement summarizing his case for Jerry's guilt. He kept the jury riveted with a combination of facts and emotional tugs. Beginning with a summary of charges, he then explored the brothers' background and their evolving relationships. The jury was hearing everything for the first time, including the legal charges against Jerry, so they listened intently. Dutton detailed Jerry's trip to Iowa in May and June of the previous year to visit the family, and his growing rage over his brother's takeover of the family business. Drawing on interviews that were taken in November and December with a variety of witnesses, including Mimi and Jerry, he was able to weave a narrative of events that led up to the murders.

Jerry's motives, Dutton stated, were a combination of revenge, jealousy, rage, and greed. Though no one could establish that Jerry sought to control the Mark family fortune, Jerry certainly seemed all but indigent. Dutton showed that he had been living off his first wife, then after their separation, he used Mimi's salary for living expenses, along with money from his parents. His odd jobs brought in very little income.

Dutton then attempted to establish that not only did Jerry have more than one motive, he had the means: the Honda 450 and that "stolen" .38 revolver which turned out to be an antique Spanish copy of a Colt handgun. And of course the rare ammunition, for which Jerry had so obligingly signed in Paso Robles.

More damning evidence had turned up since they had arrested Jerry in early November. They had subpoenaed various phone companies for call records, and just days before the records would have been destroyed, they traced Jerry's calls to Mimi in Berkeley.

Though computers were by no means as sophisticated or as powerful as today's desktop memory behemoths, large data banks were used to store records of millions of calls for billing purposes. Thanks to investigators persevering, searching through literally barrels of computer card records, they found the exact calls made to the couple's Berkeley phone number.

Dutton explained: "Although Jerry claims that he went south and arrived at about suppertime in Coalinga, California, such was not the case. He claims to have called Mimi from Coalinga upon arrival. But you will hear from a representative of the telephone company that all phone calls are recorded on a computer and that if a telephone call was made by Jerry from anywhere in or near Coalinga to a given number in or around Berkeley, there would be a record of that call. The phone company searched its records for the time, place, and numbers in question and will tell you that no such call was made."

Dutton paused to let that hard fact penetrate, then continued. "A call was in fact placed to Mimi and Jerry's apartment in Berkeley from Lovelock, Nevada, which is on a direct line from Berkeley toward the state of Iowa and the homeplace."

The prosecutor would show this disparity using a large wall map during the actual testimony. He went on, "The defendant further states that he called Mimi the next night when he was in the Provo, Utah area. Once again the phone company checked the phone records of the Provo area and you will find that no such call was made. However, a call was made to that same Berkeley number at 9:00 PM that night from Cheyenne, Wyoming. Cheyenne is 478 miles east of Provo, Utah, and that much closer to Iowa."

Gathering evidentiary steam, he proceeded to offer an overview of information about the motorcycle license plate, showing that someone had replaced the California plate with the Iowa plate at some point in the ride.

The evidence came down to grease on the license plate bolts: "A motorcycle chain, located on the left side, throws off grease which coats the parts on that side, including the bolts which hold the license plate. The bolts and parts on the opposite side are clean. The evidence will show that when Jerry put the bolts back after changing the license plates the two clean bolts which came from the right side were placed on the two top holes on the right and left. The two dirty bolts were placed on the bottom. Instead of having two clean bolts on the right side there is one clean and one dirty. Instead of two dirty bolts on the left side one is dirty and the other is clean."

During actual testimony, assistants wheeled the Honda into the courtroom so jurors could examine it for themselves, including wear marks that the disconnected odometer cable etched onto the Honda's gas tank—it had rubbed enough to make a visible indent in the paint on the tank.

Dutton ended his opening statement with a detailed explanation of Jerry Mark's arrival at the homeplace, the murderer's actions as he crept into the house, and the brutal murders. The prosecutor was illustrating why this case had mobilized so many investigators. The murdered children especially made their quest all but personal. Several members of the jury were visibly shocked and moved.

Then Dutton brought up a strange point about the crime scene photos of Jorjean's body. "As you will see from the photo," he began, "some time before she died and after she was made to lie on the floor, she extended her first two fingers from her left hand. She died with these two fingers extended from an otherwise closed hand." He was inferring that Jorjean was signaling "two," because Jerry was Les's second brother.

Explaining Jerry's ride back to Mimi's parents' house in South Lake Tahoe, Nevada, the prosecutor reminded the jury that somewhere between Iowa and Nevada, the killer had to dispose of the revolver, a white sweatshirt, and other incriminating belongs. Hence Jerry Mark thought he had committed the perfect crime—no witnesses, no on-scene evidence, and with plenty of character testimony about his deep brotherly love for Les.

Following his teams' plan, Dutton then began calling witnesses who were most familiar with Les and Jorjean. Barbara Wulf took the stand, who with her husband Dennis, had been the last people in Cedar Falls to see the Marks alive on Halloween night. Nothing especially telling there, except they were a loving and close family. Then the first two investigators took the stand telling the jury in detail the floor plan of the homeplace and where the house sat relative to the highways that led to it.

Clark Renner then took the stand. Under extended questioning he explained what time he arrived, what he saw, his refusal to enter the house alone, and his fetching of Les's parents, and the trauma that followed.

From then on, Dutton proceeded chronologically and methodically through the details of the case.

As the prosecution's case unfolded, Dutton more than fulfilled his promise to begin with a picture of the whole "puzzle." After his overview, Dutton proceeded to examine each part so it fit a completed whole. All in all, Dutton spent the next three weeks offering prosecution testimony from sixty-six witnesses, a few of whom were called back twice and even three times for further testimony and cross-examination. The most important was Leslie Warren, who claims he saw Jerry in Chappell—but a day earlier than Jerry had claimed all along. Warren testified that he worked all morning on Friday, October 31, but only for an hour the next morning, and during that time did not see anyone in the rest area. However, he insisted that he had talked with Jerry in the men's room that Friday, and was in fact able to pick him out from a line-up in Waterloo as well as from photographs.

As Warren put it, the traveler he talked to in the Chappell rest stop was polite about asking whether he could move his gear (he was washing up) and that was unusual, because "most people, from what I have observed there, pretty much do what they want to do. They don't ask about if they can do this or do that; they just do what they will."

In fact, three other eyewitnesses placed Jerry in various locations on his way to the homeplace, all of whose testimony raised questions about Jerry's continued insistence on never having biked much past the western Nebraska panhandle.

Jury members were downright startled when they heard testimony from Jack Makendonsky. Though he hadn't recognized Jerry from photographs or at a line-up, Mr. Makendonsky certainly remembered that he had talked with him about being from Iowa, and that Jerry presented his driver's license when he paid for the box of .38 caliber Long Colt bullets. Dutton queried:

"…When a person, a customer comes in to purchase ammunition, Mr. Makendonski, what procedure is followed and what kind of information is taken to record that sale?"

"Okay. We keep a book, also in chronological order, of all handgun ammunition sales, and we are required to record the name of the individual and also an identification number. Social Security or driver's license is usually what is used. And this has to be produced, and we record it."

Dutton then made sure the jury understood that those bullets were rare—the two boxes that the agents purchased in that store were the only two .38 Long Colt cartridge boxes they had seen, and Jerry had bought the only box that the store had ever sold.

The most complex testimony occurred during the FBI analyst's comparison of the spent bullets found in and around the bodies with the agent-purchased cartridges. The analyst, who worked out of Washington, DC, in the FBI laboratory, had examined all of the leads from the murder scene against a sampling of leads from the bought cartridges and offered the following for the jury: "I determined that every one of the specimens from the murder scene matched the composition of one or more of the specimens that were purchased in the shop."

Scalise did his best to refute this by pointing out that well over a hundred thousand such cartridges were manufactured that year, and any number of people might have bought a box anywhere full of cartridges with similar composition. The expert agreed that was true. Also the method that he used was "neutron activation analysis," an extremely high-tech procedure that required a nuclear reactor bombarding the lead (or any substance to be analyzed) with neutrons, a test that yielded seemingly reliable evidence of the chemical makeup of practically anything. However, some years after the trial, this method was shown to be flawed and would not have been admitted if the trial were held more recently. However, this fact was not brought up during the many appeals by either side.

Dutton's closing made Scalise shudder. Observers agreed that Dutton's rhetoric was masterful, that it added a powerful emotional dimension to the testimony. "The jury system has survived," he began, "because of the combined and collective common sense of people who were willing to confront reality and call it the way they see it, regardless of what their feelings may be. Some feelings have attempted to be engendered in you. You have got to push those down. Your decision is not to be based on sympathy or anger or passion, but on clear and calculated analysis of the evidence in this case."

Dutton knew that the jury may well have sympathized with Dorothy, whose testimony amounted to an appeal to the goodness of her family and her son. He knew he needed to remind them that decisions based on the evidence made a good verdict, not sympathy. Then he took full advantage of the mythical aspects of the murders, alluding to two well-known stories, one a fairy tale and the other Biblical.

"If you remember the story of Hansel and Gretel, you will remember that when they went on their walk, they dropped pieces of bread to mark the trail, and the birds came by and ate up the pieces of bread. So they couldn't find their way back. And the Defendant left a trail, but it was a false trail. It was a trail that he was going to use to cover his whereabouts while he slipped into Iowa to commit those murders. He dropped a piece of bread in Coalinga, California, on Wednesday evening at about 6:00, by claiming to make a phone call to his home number. But the phone company, searching its records, said, "Huh-uh, he didn't make a phone call from that location that evening." He continued to detail exactly where the calls originated to Mimi's number, according to phone company records, and he had lined up witnesses from the phone company to testify to that effect.

Then Dutton anticipated the objection that it was just too far-fetched to accuse a brother of killing a brother. "We have got a brother killing a brother. Unusual? Let me tell you a story. It's not a story that I made up. There was a man who had two sons. One son was a grain farmer and the other raised sheep. And they grew up, and one of them raised the grain and he harvested it and brought it in. The other raised the sheep and brought the sheep in. And the grain farmer felt that his grain was not considered as important as his brother's sheep, so one day when they were out in the field, the brother who was the grain farmer killed his brother the shepherd. And when he went home that night his father asked him, 'Where is your brother?' And the grain farmer said, 'I don't know where he is. And, by the way, what makes you think I am my brother's keeper?'"

Dutton paused a good while here while the jury pondered. Then: "The grain farmer's name was Cain. His brother's name was Abel. And their father was Adam. And the first story in the Old Testament tells you about two brothers, and the first story about two brothers shows one brother killing the other out of jealousy, out of hatred. So if you think that you're dealing with something unique, if you think you're dealing with something that's never happened before, consult the scriptures. It's the first story you'll find, and the first example of one brother killing another."

Then he made the connection explicit. "Let me tell you about two brothers in Cedar Falls. One brother stayed home, stayed on the farm, and he worked hard and he was devoted to his father. As a result of his hard work and his devotion, he was successful. And as his father got sick and his father became unable to care for the farm, this son took over, and this son became the fourth generation to run the farm enterprises, to be the farmer of the family."

No names were needed; the mythical quality remained intact. "And his other brother, who had the benefit of a good education, the benefit of all that the family could give him, dropped out. He went out to live on the West Coast. He went out to be unemployed and was unemployed. And while he was sitting near his trailer, talking about his family back in Iowa, he told his friend a couple of things: he said, "I did once upon a time love my brother." He said, "I cared for him. I taught him everything he knew about farming. And then when we farmed together, we couldn't get along, and my father played one of us against the other and my father preferred my brother." And he said, "My little brother screwed me out of my farm." He said, "Now I hate my brother. I can never forgive him for what he did." And he said "I told my father when I was in his presence that I would piss on his grave when he died."

Dutton closed the prosecution's case with "Ladies and gentlemen, that relationship of brother and brother, that competition for favor with the father, that jealousy, that greed, that desire, that's part of this case. It makes up the total picture." And he reminded the jury about Jerry's having consistently lied: "I think you have got to ask yourselves this question: the Defendant has two degrees, one from Iowa State and another from the University of Iowa law school. He has represented people charged with crimes. He knows the law. He knows what criminal investigators are about. I think the same statement has to be asked about the Defendant's lying to you about his whereabouts as you would ask about anyone, and that is, if he wasn't guilty, if he didn't commit the crimes, if he had nothing to hide, if his activities were normal and explainable and understandable and justifiable, why lie?"

With that phrase ringing in the courtroom, Dutton sat, and Ruxlow gave him a "well done" look that validated the special prosecutor's sense of a job well done.

The trial ended with Dutton's rebuttal of the defense's points from their closing, one by one. Since the law required that the defense didn't have to prove anything, only raise doubts about the prosecution's case, Dutton's rebuttal was par for the course. It leveled the playing field, making sure that the prosecution could at least respond to the defense's ongoing insistence on raising doubts.

He touched on every doubt and inconsistency that Scalise and Sandre had raised, particularly their attempt to generate alternative explanations. "Ladies and gentlemen, I warned you before we began that problems arise when you start asking 'what if' questions. Remember your instructions: you should not ignore credible evidence and hunt for doubt, nor should you consider arguments that are based on groundless conjecture and that cause you to engage in speculation."

He paused, knowing that he was speaking directly to the "blue car" theory that the defense had raised; one defense witness had testified that he saw a blue car leave the homeplace driveway early that morning at a high rate of speed. "Well, what if a blue car was looking at the farm, might that mean something? That's the 'what if' question. That's hunting for doubt. Turning over every rock trying to prevent you from seeing the credible evidence in the case."

He reminded them that lawyers can "argue sufficiently to cause you to wonder if you're even here; raise questions in your mind to cause you to ask the question, 'Is this a dream? Maybe I'm still at home. Maybe this is something I have just dreamed about and I will wake up and it will all be gone. This really didn't happen.' And that's a very finely polished art of adversary, and you must be careful of it."

Dutton continued, "There is nothing that I have done in this case that's made the evidence any better than it is, any different than it is. And you have heard it in its unvarnished simplicity. Look at the evidence, don't look at me. Don't consider whether I have told you anything or whether you believe what I have said or not, but look at the evidence."

Then he detailed the defense's other attempts to raise doubts, from the time of death as shown on the stopped clocks at the homeplace to the eyewitnesses' statements in Iowa about the time they saw Jerry (leaving aside any doubts that they saw him at all, which itself was a problem, since Jerry claimed to have never gotten near the homeplace) to the bullets, finishing with this:

> "Step back and look at the things the Defense didn't tell you about. Look at the bullets that he purchased on October 20, 1975. Look at the gun that he got from Alga Forrest's camper after pulling the phone wires on the trailer. Look at the license plate that's gone. Look at the lies that he told when he was asked where he was at the time of the murder. Look at all that together, and you tell me whether or not that convinces you that that Defendant is guilty of these crimes."

He then refuted Sandre's argument that Jerry had to be "crazy" to commit such heinous murders. "Don't tell me," he told the jury, "that a man is not capable of murder, even this kind of murder, without being rational. Many times that is, in fact, what the person considers to be the rational way to handle or to solve his problems. You and I may not think so, but he did."

Dutton knew it was time for a final reminder of the central facts. He continued, "The defense cannot explain the bullets. They cannot explain the gun. They cannot explain the license plate. Ladies and gentlemen, those are the very implements of the murder itself. Those are the bullets that he bought and used to kill that family. That's the gun that he used to stand point blank over each of those small children and pull the trigger twice. That's the license plate that he put on the back of the motorcycle, so he could get into Iowa. And he shaved his beard not so he wouldn't get recognized in Iowa, at his homeplace, but because he was going there under cover of darkness, but he didn't want to be recognized on the interstate. Those are the cold, hard realities of this case. They are not pleasant, but that's the state of the record."

And with that, he thanked the jury, feeling reasonably satisfied that he had made the state's case based solely on hard evidence, albeit circumstantial.

24: Trial II

LAWRENCE SCALISE AND John Sandre had conferred with Jerry for months about their strategy. The three lawyers knew they had to convince at least one juror to demand more than circumstantial evidence to convict. The standards for conviction in a criminal trial were higher than a civil suit, meaning the law was on the defendant's side. Even though there were plenty of circumstances that pointed to Jerry, they felt sure that one juror would agree that Jerry could not have murdered his brother. They remembered *Twelve Angry Men*, the 1957 film with Henry Fonda as the juror who wouldn't be convinced by mere probabilities. They needed a skeptic, a Henry Fonda character to question Dutton's evidence.

Sandre would handle the opening and both Scalise and Sandre would share the closing, the opening being more or less a routine statement of innocence, and the closing the most critical phase of the defense.

They also knew that Dutton's closing would grab and hold the jury like nothing they could muster, making it not only memorable, but newsworthy. Dutton was a master rhetorician, and they would struggle to counter his ringing phrases. It didn't help that his rhetoric was backed with so many circumstances that pointed directly to Jerry Mark.

Sandre's opening would reveal probable flaws in the prosecution's case, focusing on the need for skeptical thinking and a reminder of Jerry and Les's brotherly love.

Since Dutton's opening came first, Sandre knew the jury would be filled with Dutton's portrayal of Jerry Mark as a brutal, heartless, angry man whose claims to innocence were a sham, all the more contemptible because he kept lying in the face of overwhelming evidence.

Sandre looked straight at jury members as he began, sweeping them visually one by one.

"Ladies and gentlemen, the evidence will show that Jerry Mark took a motorcycle trip. It will further show, I believe, that that trip was planned, an arranged trip, and had been planned for some time. That he talked about it with other people; that he had considered it; that's the kind of thing that he had always wanted to do, and that it's in fact the kind of thing a lot of people would want to do. It's the kind of thing that the evidence will show is part of Jerry Mark's nature. It's the type of thing that the evidence will show is not sinister. It's the kind of thing that the evidence will show is not involved in this case, with the exception of the view put on by Mr. Dutton."

Dutton smiled at this, and kept listening for their strategy. He knew they would reveal it during this opening and follow it closely during the trial, barring some catastrophic admission or the sudden emergence of new evidence.

Sure enough, Sandre's next statement affirmed what Dutton expected. Sandre spoke, deliberately and with lawyerly sincerity:

"The evidence will show, ladies and gentlemen, that Jerry

Mark grew up in that farmhouse. That he grew up with three brothers, and he grew up with his father, Wayne, and he grew up with his mother, Dorothy. And the evidence will also show that the family worked together. The family struggled together. That family loved each other. That family had disagreements. It will show you with respect to that family what any evidence would show you with respect to any family: that there was love, that there were disagreements. It will show you nothing more than that."

Dutton groaned to himself: the loving family card. He saw the Marks as a highly dysfunctional family, and Sandre was portraying them as the Waltons with Jerry as John-Boy. Hard to refute, and Sandre was exploiting it for all it was worth.

Sandre continued: "I'm trying to show you a human situation. The evidence will show Jerry Mark in that human situation, no different than any of the other family members in that human situation.

"The evidence, ladies and gentlemen, will show a relationship between this defendant, Jerry Mark, and Les Mark. The evidence of that relationship, ladies and gentlemen, will show that they farmed together, that they worked together. The evidence will show that they had a disagreement. That's absolutely a fact.

"But the point is the evidence will also show that the substance and sum of that disagreement had to do with a brother that Mr. Dutton has mentioned by the name of Tom Mark. It had to do with the question of the provision for Tom, considering his illness, considering his difficulties, and considering the extent that that young fellow is disturbed."

Sandre knew that Jerry in fact did try to get his brothers and father to try to fund a permanent cure for Tom and that they had refused, which gave credence to their "loving brother" image of Jerry. He continued:

"The evidence will indicate that Jerry Mark took a position that had nothing to do with himself. He took a position that simply had to do with how well that other son was provided for. That's the nature of this disagreement, and that's the *sole* nature of this disagreement. And the evidence will show that that disagreement was resolved. It was resolved among the brothers, as it ought to have been, and that's what that's all about, the evidence will show."

Dutton made a mental note to possibly refute this; that disagreement was in fact never resolved, just abandoned, as were so many of the Mark family disagreements. Sandre then mentioned the weaknesses in the prosecution's case concerning blood typing on a cigarette butt, where a deputy's cigarette butt was found to have been smoked by a "Type O" person, which was Jerry's blood type, and they might have tried to show that the butt had been smoked by him, but the typing test was subject to error. And the lead from the found slugs, Sandre asserted, could not have been the lead from the cartridges that Jerry had bought. As he put it, "when you hear that evidence, it will provide you with the answer as to whether or not those bullets came from the same batch… we feel that the evidence will show that they did not; that they *clearly* did not."

Sandre then returned to their major tactic: Jerry's sterling character and family ties. "Ladies and gentlemen, Jerry Mark was born on that farm. He grew up on that farm. He grew up with those brothers. He had a special relationship with Les, a special kind of relationship other than the one we feel that you have heard described here earlier. The evidence will show that Jerry Mark loved Les Mark; that Jerry loved those children. The evidence will show that he loves his own children in an extraordinary kind of way."

"In addition to growing up on the farm and attending Cedar Falls schools, he attended Iowa State University as well as the University of Iowa law school. Between all those times, ladies and gentlemen, Jerry Mark was one of the original members of the Peace Corps, President John Kennedy's Peace Corps. He traveled to Brazil and spent something on the order of two years there working with the poor, bringing that kind of knowledge to them that he had from growing up on the farm. And then when he returned from there, ladies and gentlemen, he traveled around; he made speeches at schools and he made speeches to the Legislature. The evidence will show these kinds of things about Jerry Mark, and you have not heard them, and the evidence will show that."

Scalise was beginning to wish that his partner would lose that "evidence will show" phrase, but knew that repetition was a major weapon in their rhetorical armory, so vowed not to admonish him.

Sandre continued:

"The evidence will show that Jerry worked with the people of Brazil. The evidence will show that when he got back and when he went to law school and got out, he worked with the people of Des Moines. In the truest and purest sense of the word, he worked with the people of Des Moines." That was a reference to Jerry's work as a legal aid lawyer in Des Moines, where he worked for practically nothing defending indigent clients.

Dutton could no longer remain silent. He interrupted Sandre's opening with "Your Honor, I'm going to have to object. The character testimony, if it's to be introduced, must be introduced only with regard to character traits that are involved in the trial; that is, truth and veracity, or character traits for violence and the type of actions that are involved in the crime. To refer to character as a result of good deeds is both inappropriate and refers to evidence that if offered during the trial would be inadmissible, and for that reason, I'm constrained to object."

Sandre wasn't surprised and felt prepared to refute. He jumped in before the judge could sustain or overrule the objection.

"Your Honor, can I respond to that?"

The judge nodded yes, and Sandre insisted that Dutton's opening statement concerned Jerry's life history, therefore he felt justified in bringing up other aspects of Jerry's life that Dutton had ignored, namely Jerry's model citizen behavior, all of which was true.

The judge agreed, asserting that it was impossible to sort out which comments to allow and disallow when it came to life histories. Sandre took the opportunity to make a point about the facts of the case and how they should be used.

"Ladies and gentlemen, perhaps that objection was the best thing that could have happened at this time. It highlighted the purpose of an opening statement. Nothing highlights it better than that objection, so we all need to remember that you folks hear and decide the facts. I'm up here telling you what facts I think are important, what they are going to prove to be, and Mr. Dutton does the same thing for you. But you make your own individual judgment and analysis of those facts, as the Court has told you."

Sandre realized that he was beginning to push the edges of "brief," so wrapped it up.

"Ladies and gentlemen, in addition to what I have tried to tell you, we believe the facts will show a couple of things we believe were directly related to the question you have to resolve: that is, did Jerry Mark enter that house and did he kill those people? We believe the evidence will show that those folks were murdered. They were murdered brutally and unfortunately and with no cause. We believe that the evidence will show that the person who murdered those four innocent individuals has an identifiable set of fingerprints, and that those fingerprints are present and that those fingerprints are not Jerry Mark's. And that the individual who murdered those four people has identifiable hair by way of type and color and that's present, and those don't belong to Jerry Mark."

Dutton made another note: speak to fingerprint evidence. Another doubt he had to dispel, although it was impossible to prove a negative—no fingerprints of Jerry's, therefore he couldn't have been there, or put another way: other fingerprints, therefore Jerry is innocent. "Non sequitur" he noted.

Sandre finished with a flourish. "The evidence will show, ladies and gentlemen, that those people were killed, and they were killed by someone other than Jerry Mark. So please do what we asked you before: at this most difficult time, keep an open mind, to think of what we have told you, and think of it in terms of a chart, a roadmap for where things are going, to listen to the evidence for yourself and evaluate it and be the judges of the facts."

And with that, he took his seat, happy to have let "facts" be his last word, and reasonably sure that his opening statement gave the jury reason to question some of the facts that Dutton's team was marshalling.

The defense strategy was to keep objecting to Dutton's evidence on the grounds that since Jerry was innocent, people who claimed to have seen him on the motorcycle did not establish his guilt, only that he was riding a motorcycle. That's not a crime, they kept insisting.

The defense's case rested first on Jerry's character, and they carried it forward with a vengeance when they put Dorothy Mark in the witness chair. Scalise knew he could count on Dorothy to make a lasting impression on the jury. When he asked whether he had told her that morning to come to the witness stand and tell the truth, she replied: "You told me that, but it wouldn't have made one bit of difference. I tell the truth."

As to her background, Scalise had her explain that she had been an elementary school teacher, she had met Wayne when he was a school bus driver, and they had been married over 38 years. And now he was dying of cancer, and had struggled with the disease for years. In response to Scalise's questions, she reminded the jury that Jerry and Les had grown up as best friends, that they had each been best man at the other's wedding, and that Jerry and Les's children had played together.

When the children playing together came up, Dutton again objected, and the judge sustained it as irrelevant, but the point had been made: Jerry was a father and a family man. Scalise then played a trump card: had Jerry and Les argued during that summer visit? Yes, but it wasn't about farming or how Les and Wayne were running the family operation, it was about how to care for Tom. Seems that all the brothers were left the same amount—$50,000, and Jerry was sure Tom would need more than all of them put together, especially if they sought a cure. Les had disagreed, she said, and they had yelled at each other about it, but "Les had yelled the loudest."

Scalise asked rhetorically why Jerry was so concerned about getting Tom extra family money, and she stated, "Jerry didn't want any money. He's never cared about money. He wasn't talking about himself; he was talking about the care given for Tom and the provisions made for Tom." She declared that that disagreement was resolved quickly, and the family went back to loving each other.

Dutton then cross-examined her, and she gave a powerful reply to his question about her state of mind:

"And this is a difficult time for you, isn't it, Mrs. Mark?"

"You mean your questioning me is difficult for me?"

"No."

"It is not."

"I meant the whole experience is difficult."

"The murder of Les and Jorjean, yes, is very difficult for me."

"Yes."

"And the accusation of my son Jerry is very difficult for me. But your questioning, Mr. Dutton, please go ahead. I want to answer any questions that will help."

Dutton felt a spark of admiration for Dorothy's ability to not only deflect his questions, but also to turn them to Jerry's advantage. She would have made a great lawyer or politician, he thought as he finished his examination, making little headway against her unshakable belief in her son's innocence.

Two weeks into the trial, with the prosecution still calling witnesses, Scalise kept pressing Jerry about taking the stand and telling his story. The former Attorney General of Iowa knew that outside of a barrage of objections to the prosecution's case, he hadn't been able to present real evidence that might give the jurors pause, nor was he able to effectively rebut much of the circumstantial evidence. Jerry needed to take the stand and refute all that evidence as best he could.

Scalise would ask Jerry to detail his alibi, and would coach Jerry on how to make it convincing, appealing to the jury's difficulty with believing that anyone so polite and well-spoken as Jerry could murder his beloved brother's family.

So Scalise confronted Jerry directly as the time to testify approached. "Jerry, you need to let me know. Dutton will be wrapping it up soon, and so will I. You need to take the stand. We've hinted you'll do that all along." Scalise looked Jerry straight in the eye, something he seldom did. Though Jerry had no legal obligation to tell his story, and his refusal could not be held against him, in this case it was his best hope.

Jerry had been dreading this day. He knew he had to make his case and let the chips fall where they may. If he did well, pulling out all the stops, maybe weeping a bit over his deceased brother and his beautiful family, talking about how he never has understood how he could be accused, much less arrested, he could pull it off. He would rail at Dutton, calling the trial a terrible miscarriage of justice due to a few coincidences and misunderstandings and overzealous cops and prosecutors. He would probably have to admit that he lied, but he wouldn't have to say exactly why.

He would put on a show and one juror would surely buy it. Hell, maybe more than one. And he'd be free.

He looked at Scalise just as directly. "All right, Larry. I'll do it. Put me on the stand tomorrow." Scalise nodded in relief and began making notes for coaching him.

Back at the hotel he told Mimi he would take the stand. She was overjoyed. She felt sure that his testimony would be the key to his freedom, as did his mother, and they were anxious to hear his whole story, from his own perspective at last. They ate together, as they usually did, in the hotel restaurant, and felt a small sense of relief that the trial was almost over, that Jerry was about to be vindicated. They retired to their rooms almost joyfully, and Mimi fell asleep quickly, relaxed and relieved.

Jerry, however, lay wide awake as waves of fear and panic washed over him. When he finally managed to doze off, another dream broke through his well-walled psyche. It became one of the more intense dreams he could remember, and it affected him immediately when he stirred awake.

In his dream, he finally took the witness stand, confident in his well-fitting three-piece blue suit, striped yellow and red tie. Ready to shine. After the oath, with his emphatic "I do" answer, he took Scalise's first question. "Jerry Mark, tell us your whereabouts on October 31 and November 1, 1975."

Modulating his voice so it sounded utterly sincere and forceful, dream-Jerry began to fight for his freedom.

"Everyone in this room deserves to hear my story, and I'm thankful for this opportunity. On the morning of October 31, I was out in western Nebraska, riding my motorcycle, enjoying my day on the road. I was making progress in finding my life's direction."

Dream-Jerry felt cooler as he spoke, and he could feel the jury actively listening, hearing him for the first time. "I'm ashamed to admit that I lied to the investigators, but I had my reasons, and they have nothing to do with murdering anyone. I'd prefer to keep them private, in fact, and won't speak any more about it, except to say that I did nothing illegal. I realized late that day that I needed to get back to California, and stayed overnight around Chappell, Nebraska, woke up around 8:00, washed up, rode the bike down the road a bit further to fill up, then turned around and headed to Cheyenne, Wyoming. That's what I was doing, and whoever was murdering my brother and his family must be ecstatic that I'm on trial here for it while they go free, and for all I know, are out there murdering again."

Dream-Jerry paused and let that sink in. Now he felt sure he was home free. Just a few softball questions from his lawyers and a quick cross-examination from Dutton, and he could rest easy.

Dream-Scalise asked him to elaborate on a few details of his trip back to California that weekend, then looked at Dream-Dutton. "Your witness."

In Jerry's dream, Dutton approached Jerry and paused, looking directly at him, then the jury.

"Jerry, you're trained as an attorney, and you received reasonably high grades in law school, am I right?"

"Yes, sir."

"And you took courses in criminal law and procedures and worked in legal aid, representing members of American Indian groups on criminal matters, and in fact studied constitutional law, did you not?"

"Yes, that's right."

"And you know that when police are conducting a criminal investigation they start with a warning that you have a right to remain silent, that anything you say can and will be used against you in a court of law, and that if you can't afford an attorney one will be appointed for you at state expense, and that you can stop answering questions at any time. You understand and understood all this, right?"

"Yes, Mr. Dutton." Out of the corner of dream-Jerry's eye he could see Scalise scowl.

"Now, you were interviewed by BCI agents as part of their investigation into your brother's death, and you were advised of your rights at that time, am I right?"

"Yes, I was."

So as an attorney yourself you know the consequences and implications of lying to the police, and you agreed to make a statement after the murders on November 3rd and November 7th, again, am I right?"

"Well, Mr. Dutton, I was not read my rights on November 3rd since I was not even remotely a suspect. But on November 7th, yes, I heard my rights read."

"All right. When you were interviewed, you did lie to the investigators who had read you your rights. You lied, in fact, about the basic facts in the investigation. You lied about where you were during that whole week. You were not in Coalinga, or Barstow, a little bird didn't wake you up there and make you decide to go on over to Las Vegas. You lied about how far east you rode, for we have witnesses who have positively identified you as being in eastern Nebraska, then in Iowa at several towns on the way to the Homeplace, all the way to Ackley, just 35 miles from your brother's home."

Dream-Scalise couldn't let this pass. "Objection, your Honor, the prosecution isn't asking a question."

"Sustained. Please get to a question, Mr. Dutton ."

"Thank you, I will, your Honor. So, Mr. Mark, are you saying that someone else using your social security number was in Paso Robles and bought those cartridges, which happen to be the same kind of rare .38 caliber Long Colt cartridges used to kill your brother and his family?" And he paused. The courtroom remained dead quiet.

Jerry wasn't sure what to say. If "yes," no one would believe in such an outlandish coincidence. If "no" he would have to launch into an explanation of why, in fact, he had bought those cartridges that would probably not fit any of the street radicals' weapons, a fact that Dutton would surely bring up.

He couldn't answer. And he knew many more such questions were coming, about the wear marks on the motorcycle, about why he consistently lied about his whereabouts and even about having bought any cartridges at all. He couldn't answer any of them without seeming like a complete fool and liar, in fact a malicious liar. In other words, he would prove himself guilty not only to the jury, but to his mother and wife. And to the world. That meant prison as a child-killer.

Untenable. Impossible.

Jerry's dream became his worst nightmare. He sprang awake, sweating. There was no way.

When Mimi awoke, he began quietly weeping.

"Jerry, what's wrong? We thought you were ready."

"That goddamn Dutton," he blubbered. "He's going to make me look like a liar and a killer. There's nothing I can say from the stand that will change that. They've got me."

"Now, Jerry, that's nerves. Take the stand and defend yourself. Otherwise, Larry told you, you're done. You've rehearsed this all. Please, Jerry. You'll go to prison for the rest of your life." She was horrified.

"I can't. I'm sorry. I'll tell Mom. Maybe I can make a statement after Scalise closes. But I'm not going to sit there and take questions that will make me look like I murdered Les."

Mimi had no answer, and neither did Dorothy a few minutes later when he called her, then Scalise. Scalise just sighed loudly and hung up.

Jerry's last hope came from Scalise and Sandre's closing statements. Sandre had insisted that he add a closing too, since Jerry wasn't going to take the stand. However, Jerry made it clear to both of them that he wanted to make a statement as well, since he could in fact act as co-counsel and could have done that from the beginning. That way he could make his case without having to submit to cross-examination.

Dutton objected strenuously. In the judge's chambers he argued that Jerry would be giving testimony, not just an argument, and "to allow him now in a closing argument to testify without being subjected to cross-examination seems to me to violate the whole spirit of the privilege that he is afforded under the Fifth Amendment to the Constitution. I see that as a way of circumventing the subjecting of his testimony to scrutiny, and it's in essence a denial of guilt in argument that he refused to make from the witness stand while under oath. And he has not appeared as counsel in this case; has not participated in any way; he has not filed an appearance and notice of his being of counsel in this case. To allow him now to appear as counsel on his own behalf after the Defense has rested is inappropriate and improper, and he should not be allowed to do so."

Judge Engelkes, erring on the side of caution, did not issue an opinion then, but let closing arguments begin, and during another conference, Scalise and Sandre withdrew Jerry's request, saying that Jerry had decided not to address the jury after all. The Judge noted this with relief, since there was no clear precedent for what Jerry was requesting, and he would have to be vigilant to make sure his comments did not amount to testimony without cross-examination.

Jerry had felt just a taste of what facing Dutton would be like when he heard Dutton's objection, and knew that his testimony wouldn't stand up against a rebuttal. He remembered his terrible dream and felt relieved when he realized that he could—and must—remain silent throughout the closings. There was still hope, thanks to his silence.

Scalise began his closing with an unusually direct compliment to Dutton, telling jurors that "you have been privileged to hear probably one of the finest lawyers you will ever hear in Mr. Dutton." And in fact he said the same of the jury, and "I want to thank them publicly for their participation and their attention and their hard work." When Jerry told Dorothy later about Scalise's compliment, Dorothy was furious. "What was he thinking?" she growled, to no one in particular.

Dutton would never express such admiration for Scalise, so this amounted to kind of a compliment one-upmanship. The prosecutor in fact dismissed it as a rhetorical ploy.

Scalise's closing brought home the point that despite a mountain of evidence and testimony, the prosecution still hadn't shown that Jerry Mark actually committed the murders. It showed only that there was a probability that he did—but mere probability was not enough. "Beyond a reasonable doubt" as a legal standard called for certainty. So Scalise hammered away at inconsistencies in the eyewitness testimonies, the fact that Mimi's ex-husband felt nothing but bitterness and contempt for Jerry and therefore gave tainted testimony against Jerry, and a litany of issues with the footprint and bullet lead lots evidence.

Then he tried a trick. He looked at the jury dead-on and implored: "If you pause, if you hesitate in reaching a full and abiding conviction of guilt, then Jerry Mark is innocent and you must vote that way, because that's what the law says. If you pause and hesitate, then you do have a reasonable doubt, and you must acquit the defendant. That's the law of Iowa."

Dutton was startled. What the hell was this? He quickly rose: "Your Honor, I object. That's an improper statement of the law and it should not be allowed to be used to confuse this jury." The judge sustained it, and Scalise backed off. He had tried to get jurors to believe that just pausing to consider the evidence carefully should be construed as doubt. Dutton cut that line of argument off, clean.

Scalise then played his most powerful card: Dorothy Mark. He began by reminding the jury that she continued to insist that Jerry was innocent. "She knows Jerry better than anybody. She knows his strengths and weaknesses better than anyone. She knows his love for his family better than anyone. I tell you, ladies and gentlemen, she knows what a son can do and what a son cannot do better, for God's sake, better than any ex-husband. She is the mother of the victims. And I tell you very sincerely that she knows in her heart her son Jerry Mark better than you do, better than Lawrence Scalise does, better than David Dutton does, better than any person in this whole courtroom. I tell you, she was here for him. She loves him with all of her heart, and no one knows the children really better than a mother. They spend most of their time with them. No one knows what he or she can and cannot do. And she knows better than anybody else that Jerry Mark could not kill Les and Jorjean and Jeff and Julie."

There it was, and Dutton had been expecting it. A raw, naked appeal to a mother's love and devotion. Dutton wondered when he should cut Scalise off. The persevering defense lawyer continued:

"You know, those kids were truly beautiful, and I have to say to you that the killing of those two is really the ultimate craziness, just the most monstrous, cruel, vicious, mean, rotten act that I have ever been witness to in any court. And we are not, I'm going to tell you, insensitive to that. We know that, just as you do. Dorothy Mark knows it even better. And what does she say to you? She says to you that Wayne is dying, Tom is ill, Les is dead, and Jerry is accused of it. She says, 'Is it hard, Mr. Dutton, to answer your questions? No. Is it hard for me that Les is murdered and Jerry is unjustly accused? That's very hard, Mr. Dutton.' You know why that's very hard, ladies and gentlemen? Because she knows best. Better than you and I and anybody else. She told you something else, too. She said it to you that she loves Jerry. She wants him home. She has reached her verdict, you see."

Dutton could not let this pass. "Your Honor, this is again improper. It's not proper argument. It's a crass appeal to sympathy, and I object to it."

The judge, surprised that Dutton had let Scalise continue so long, sustained the objection, but Scalise felt pleased that he could appeal at last to the jury's powerful feelings for family ties. He then made his final comment, adding "moral" to "certainty" to give it weight. "I want you to know that in our view, proof of guilt must be to a moral certainty, beyond a reasonable doubt. That's what it means. And I do not think that proof that Jerry Mark was present on those premises, pulled the trigger and killed those people, and even, in fact, shot them after they were dead, rises even to the level of probability. And even if it does, you have got to acquit him, because that's the law of the State of Iowa. I'm going to ask you to follow it. Please do that. And if you do, you will acquit Jerry Mark."

And he sat, feeling he had done all he could do by continuing to introduce the point of "moral certainty" and reasonable doubt. Jerry nodded "well done" to him, hoping the jury was buying it. Then Sandre made the defense's final closing statement, mostly repeating what Scalise had said, though avoiding bringing up Dorothy's love for her sons.

He reminded the jury that Jerry stood accused of not only killing his brother's family, but also killing them in a horribly vengeful way. He asserted that Jerry simply was not capable of such aberrant behavior, and Dutton thought "red herring," as he had many times while listening to Sandre and Scalise.

Sandre wrapped his closing up with "Ladies and gentlemen, having Jerry Mark sitting here accused is a tragedy upon a tragedy, and I ask you, with respect to that, simply this: that before we perpetuate and compound that tragedy, be satisfied beyond a reasonable doubt, to a moral certainty, and demand more from this evidence than the possibility that he could have, and more than even probability. As Jerry Mark has said to an investigator, when shown the pictures of his murdered niece and nephew, 'I beg you, please don't stop looking.'"

And with that, Sandre and Scalise's defense rested. Jerry, Mimi, and Dorothy felt hopeful. One skeptical juror would save him.

25: Verdict

JUDGE ENGELKES GAVE the jury their instructions and dismissed them for deliberation late in the afternoon, and the next morning on June 22, 1976, received a note that the twelve men and women had reached a verdict. They had deliberated around five hours. He immediately called the court into session at 11:20 AM, and the large crowd was allowed to enter the courtroom. All were surprised that the jury had reached a verdict so quickly; capital murder cases usually took far longer.

Scalise had returned to Des Moines the night before, and Dorothy fumed about that too. Complimenting Dutton! Leaving the trial before the verdict! She was taken aback that Scalise seemed so cavalier about her son's fate. Sandre and Jerry took their usual places, as did Dutton, Ruxlow, David Correll, and Harry Zanville. The courtroom silence was palpable. Jerry tried to hope for the best. He and Sandre knew that a quick verdict in a murder case boded ill.

Gaveling the court into session, Judge Engelkes ordered the jury into the courtroom to deliver their verdict. Jerry was told to stand and the judge, having just read the verdict, looked straight at him and spoke.

"The verdict of the Jury in each of the four cases reads as follows"—and he nodded at the foreman, who took over and intoned the traditional phrasing:

"We, the Jury, find the defendant guilty of four counts of murder in the first degree."

The hundred and fifty or so relatives, spectators, and reporters let out a collective gasp. Mimi and Dorothy seemed overcome with shock, and hung their heads in unison. They expected only exoneration.

Dutton and his team shook hands and beamed, while Sandre stared at the table, betraying no emotion. Jerry's face glowed his usual red, but otherwise he remained passive. He feared this was coming; he had conferred with Scalise and Sandre the night before, and Scalise had informed him that Dutton's rhetoric probably had overwhelmed the jury. He didn't bring up all the evidence they couldn't refute, nor did he remind Jerry that his not taking the stand to tell his own story was a fatal error.

"Jerry," Scalise had advised, "Don't overreact. Everyone will be watching. Don't act guilty. Take it with dignity and keep in mind the appeals process. This isn't over." Jerry knew Scalise and Sandre felt they had done all they could, but he still felt utterly betrayed. He needed better lawyers.

Turning to Sandre, the judge asked, "Do you wish to have the jury polled?" Sandre nodded yes, and each juror stood to answer, "yes" when asked, "Are these your true verdicts?" The judge then instructed the BCI agents who had accompanied Jerry into the courtroom every day to remand Jerry into custody, and withdrew bail "pending further order of the court."

Sandre was planning to file an appeal almost immediately, so he rose, saying, "Your Honor, may the record reflect our exception to this ruling of the court?" The judge agreed to note that objection as a matter of procedure.

The judge knew that he needed to return the case to Black Hawk County for sentencing, and Sandre agreed that there was no need for the entire operation to remain in Sioux City. The sentencing was set for the second week of July at the Black Hawk County courtroom, and Jerry was led out in handcuffs. Dorothy and Mimi tearfully watched him go, and prepared to drive back to Cedar Falls without him.

After reporters and spectators left the courtroom, and with Dutton, Ruxlow, and Sandre still present, Judge Engelkes offered informal but on-the-record comments. In effect, he complimented everyone associated with the case, including the media, the jury themselves, and both the prosecution and defense. In his own words, "I just think that we all have to recognize the criminal justice system and the whole procedure of criminal justice in our country is really in good hands. You have seen it operating at its very best. You have seen counsel, both for the State and for the Defense, rendering the kind of performance of the professional tasks in a manner that I think we all must agree has been of the highest quality."

He even complimented Ron Abrahamson, the intrepid court reporter, who had taken nearly 3200 pages of testimony with no relief or back-up, and the media, who had reported on the trial for the major Iowa newspaper dailies and TV stations. He finished with "I think everyone deserves the very highest accolades for the quality of the performance that has gone on here. I hope as you look back on this experience, the difficult experience you have had, those thoughts will fade in your memory, and what will remain are the recollections of all the very good kinds of memories that you will want to keep and talk about."

In fact, though Engelkes couldn't fully register his approval of the verdict, he appreciated the skillful combination of investigative work and legal talent that allowed a conviction to emerge from wholly circumstantial evidence. He felt confident that the appeals which were sure to follow would support this trial fully.

By the evening news cycle, reporters picked up on Dutton's characterization of the case as the "Cain and Abel" murders, and that tag stuck. For his part, Jerry knew his life would now narrow to a lifer's cell until he could find the right loophole. Though both Scalise and Sandre encouraged him to stay positive, he knew how long appeals could take. There were several glitches in the trial, as there always were, but probably nothing that rose to the level of an immediate mistrial. In fact, Dutton's team and the judge bent over backwards to assure there were no legal grounds for a successful appeal.

That night, Jerry slept in the Woodbury County jail, and was allowed one phone call, which he made to his mother, knowing Mimi would be nearby. After a short exchange of regrets and sorrys to his mother, Jerry consoled Mimi. But she needed to vent.

"Jerry, I'm so scared for you. And me. What's going to happen? If you had taken the stand, could you have won? I'm confused, and your mom is furious with everyone and everything. What should we do?"

He had to let her rail on. She could visit him in the Black Hawk County jail after they returned, but now he needed to try to comfort her.

"Mimi, I know how you feel. Just remember lots of cases are won on appeal. You know I got screwed, and Scalise is still one of the best lawyers in the Midwest. He told me last night not to lose heart. We'll appeal it right away and I shouldn't have to do much time. We have lots of ideas about this, and these guys know what we have to do."

"Yeah, but shall I go back to Berkeley? Shall I wait for your sentencing? Your mother wants me to stay, but I can't keep living off your family. Jerry, I really thought you'd be acquitted."

"Yeah, me too, but that's the way these things work." A tense silence followed. Jerry broke it with, "Because it looks so bad, the jury gets swayed, and I have to prove myself on appeal. But it will happen, I know. We'll be back in Berkeley by the end of the year. You know that's true. I love you, Mimi, and I'll see you back in Waterloo. You've gotta have faith."

They hung up, and Jerry spent the rest of the day stewing. He knew his family could afford appeals, and he knew Mimi would wait awhile. But not forever. How long, and who could he really talk to about any of this?

Throughout the trial he had watched Dutton unfold the case against him with fascination and horror. They really had done the investigative legwork he assumed they would never do. Those goddamn bullets. How in hell did they find out so fast? And why had he signed his real name, for god's sake? He had been terrified they would find his stash, but they hadn't and probably never would. Relief there at least. And those phone calls. Jesus Christ. Who would ever have thought they'd keep computer records to his Berkeley number from pay phones along the Interstate? He was screwed. Then that Honda, with paint on the gas tank all rubbed away. Son of a bitch. He couldn't stop shaking his head and cursing, though he kept it low; he knew jailers would pass on any signs of emotional instability to their superiors.

His big problem: what to do about his parents and Mimi? If they stopped believing him he was sunk, plain and simple. Not to mention his lawyers. At least Sandre seemed willing to carry on.

They brought him a jail dinner, and he ate knowing it would be the first of many state-issue meals: Tough hamburger, barely warmed frozen peas, stale bread, iceberg lettuce, and sour coffee. He had had his last decent meal the night before in the hotel and remembered it ruefully: steak and a baked potato, Caesar salad.

He lay down, restless but strangely relieved. At least he now knew his life's direction. He would show the bastards. Dutton was wrong, his whole prosecution strategy fatally flawed. Cain and Abel, for Christ's sake. The nerve. He dozed, that jailhouse dinner not going down quietly, the lack of privacy already making him wonder about being under lock and key. So unjust, so wrong, he kept telling himself.

As he slipped into sleep, the day's events came back as a surreal train of images that he failed to control. At first he awakened in their Berkeley apartment, went outside to look at his interstate-ready Honda, shook his head, and walked back in and noticed the date. Wednesday, October 29. He again shook his head and remembered that he was scheduled to work at some odd jobs for his landlord that day. So he dressed for work instead of a long ride. What a crazy idea that was anyway, he told himself, amazed that he had taken it so far as to actually buy a box of cartridges and a riding suit.

Then he struggled awake enough to see the bars, and realized he had entered and left the parallel universe of lucid dreaming. Then he dozed again, and another vision arrived, this time taking him straight back to that July cornfield. He found himself in the middle of that field, but now it was mid-winter. The harvested, stubble acres of corn were lightly dusted with snow, and a sharp wind whirled. He stood on ground as hard as concrete, with frozen topsoil visible to the horizon. No distinguishing features. Just the low roll of a harvested Iowa field unbroken by fencerows or trees. It was freezing; the wind sliced. Wearing no warm clothes, he did not move to warm himself. He could only stand and watch snow swirl and whip around him. Jerry Mark morphed into a sculpture, frozen and rooted deep into the dark Iowa landscape.

26. Appeals

JERRY MARK'S FIRST appeal went to the Iowa Supreme Court in 1979. He felt sure that he, Scalise and Sandre had made a powerful case that the eyewitnesses had been coached, misinformed, and downright misled, and that Dutton's team had withheld evidence that would exonerate him.

The Iowa Supreme Court would have none of it. On December 19, 1979, they issued their opinion: appeal denied. They could find no evidence of judicial or prosecutorial wrongdoing, and they affirmed the procedures and the verdict.

Jerry was beside himself. How could they have dismissed it so casually, without even a hearing? Surely the judges could see what he,

Scalise, and Sandre knew: all the evidence was circumstantial, and good lawyers can pick holes in anything without hard evidence. Jerry knew it was just a matter of time before he found a sympathetic judge. That's how the law works, as he not only had learned, but had experienced, both as a legal aid lawyer and as a victim of a zealous prosecutor.

So he kept trying. Though the law library at "The Fort"—Iowa's maximum security prison in Fort Madison—was limited, and he couldn't spend more than a couple of hours a week there, thanks to limited time and space, he managed to craft an extended appeal of the Supreme Court's denial.

By early 1980, he had not only filed an extensive appeal, he had written a protest letter in which he threatened non-violent protest which he hoped would end in his death, either by starvation or by shooting during an escape attempt.

As he put it, "I simply will use my life to exercise disobedience against an imprisonment which is both legally and morally wrong. Illegal detention of an innocent man degrades the human values of all people. All ought to abhor the injustice I am suffering."

Of course some did abhor his imprisonment, among them his parents, though Wayne admitted later that he thought Jerry had lied to him. Some old friends and the family ministers, stayed loyal to Dorothy, who simply could not believe that Jerry was in prison on four counts of murder. One of the worst mass murders in Iowa history up to then, no less.

Mimi, meanwhile, stuck by him for two years, but by the time of the first appeal, Jerry was single again. Before the divorce, she filed two suits, one for false imprisonment, referring to her November 1975 time in jail before they arrested Jerry, and another suit for harassment against the police who interrogated her. Both suits were dismissed as having no merit. When I spoke to her briefly on the telephone in 1980, she told me cryptically, "Everything you want to know about the Mark murders, Jerry Mark can tell you." However, I was not able to pursue that idea nor undertake a full interview because more appeals were pending, and Jerry's lawyer at the time, John Sandra, would not grant permission for an interview.

Jerry ranted and fumed and kept insisting he had been imprisoned illegally by "Ayatollahs" who deserved contempt for their betrayal of legal and moral principles. Because his family still controlled a considerable fortune, he retained various lawyers who were able to continue his quest for exoneration. When I visited with him in 1980 in Fort Madison, he vented against his father for not allowing the defense to bring in evidence that Wayne's Vi-Vim corporation had taken advantage of older people's ignorance of real estate values. Both Leo Baker and Bill Sindlinger were in fact disbarred for their association with Wayne and his shady real estate dealings. (See "Sources," Chapter 26 for the facts of that story.) Jerry felt that the jury would have found a motive for killing both Les and his father had they heard that evidence during his trial.

Jerry also fussed to me about Scalise not letting him take the stand, that he wanted to tell his story for the jury, but Scalise would not allow him. When I mentioned this to Scalise the next day in Des Moines, he asked, "Is that what he told you? Listen, I told Jerry Mark that if he did not take the stand, he would be convicted, and he decided he couldn't, that Dutton would take him apart."

I asked Lawrence Scalise if he thought his former client was guilty, and he just smiled, saying, "Let's just say there were questions he couldn't answer."

Other appeals in the 1980s and 1990s were also denied and until 2006, most people who knew the case figured that Jerry Mark had exhausted any possibility of exoneration. Then in August of 2006, 8th District Circuit Court of Appeals Judge Donald O'Brien ordered that Jerry Mark be set free or retried. As O'Brien put it, "This court is not ruling that Mark is not guilty of the crimes, only that in a careful detailed review of the cumulative effect of all the evidence that was not disclosed, Mark did not receive a fair trial."

Dorothy, very much alive, and others who never stopped believing in Mark's innocence, felt elated and vindicated. Ruxlow and Dutton, among others, wondered whether they were going to have to dust off 30-year-old evidence and search out witnesses, some of whom had died, all of whom would have to be extensively re-interviewed.

The state of Iowa appealed Judge O'Brien's ruling, and assistant Iowa Attorney Thomas Ewald wrote the state's case, asserting essentially that the bulk of the evidence presented during the trial offered overwhelming proof of guilt, and that Mark's continuing use of appeals relied on relatively minor discrepancies in eyewitness testimony and barely useable DNA evidence, none of which provided an alibi. The one possible exception was Leslie Warren's inability to testify exactly when he saw Jerry Mark at the rest stop in Chappell. However, all available evidence other than Warren's doctor's office record showed Warren in the doctor's office Friday morning. Therefore he could not have seen Mark on Saturday, far enough from the murder scene to provide an alibi. However, even Mark admitted in an early interview that he traveled to Chappell on Friday, discrediting his own story.

A panel of three judges heard the State's case. They questioned Assistant Attorney General Ewald about Jean Doyle, an eyewitness who would have provided an alibi had she been reliable, but who was shown to live in a somewhat delusional world, and the Leslie Warren records. In the end the three judges agreed fully with the state's case, writing on August 16, 2007 that "For the foregoing reasons, we reverse the district court's grant of Mark's petition for write of *habeus corpus* and affirm its denial of his motion to expand the record. On remand, we instruct the district court to enter an order denying Mark's petition with prejudice."

Jerry Mark did not attend this hearing, having run out of funds to either pay attorneys or travel to trial venues.

As of this writing in June, 2011, Jerry Mark, now 69, is completing the 35th year of his four consecutive life terms in the Iowa State Penitentiary, still creating appeals, still seeking exoneration.

PART 2: SOURCES

Introduction to Sources

BROTHER'S BLOOD is primarily a nonfiction story, with interludes of fictional recreation of conversations, personal thoughts and dreams. As a nonfiction story, readers may appreciate knowing my sources. I offer them unedited except for elisions and original errors marked "sic," letting them stand on their own as information readers can use to form their own decisions as to the accuracy of the story.

I had no access to sources for family conversations, dreams, or thoughts of any of the people. Those details I fictionalized in order to create a readable and engaging narrative. My fictionalized account may be close to the truth, but this remains a mystery as I do not and could not have known what literally occurred. However, all events, places, people, and place names are based on fact. From my experience even those who experienced the events have differing memories, so the past always remains ambiguous—part fact, part imagined fiction.

I trust readers will understand the need for poetic license, even when real people are involved, in order to create a story from what is essentially a series of reports, transcripts, newspaper stories, and interviews— the raw material on which I drew. In other words, connections to real persons, living and dead, is intended throughout, though tentative at times due to the inevitable gulf between third person observing and first person knowledge, or an absence of factual material upon which to draw.

Scott Cawelti,
February, 2011

1. Revolver

On November 7, 1975, police interviewed Jerry Mark at the Cedar Falls Police Department. Here is his explanation of how he found the revolver:

JM: …we had some fishing poles and a…revolver that belonged to her husband down there—It was a six-shooter type revolver and it was—I assume it was around a .38 caliber or something because it was, you know, it was a lot bigger than a .22 caliber

Interviewer: Did you ever have occasion to handle it?

JM: No, well, I handled it—I'll tell you the only time I really handled it was when we got it—when we got this revolver was when—when they split up and he wouldn't let her have any of her stuff… I helped her get the camper and he [Alga] had pulled this gun on her once and—uh—this—this is really the only time I handled the gun at all—but we—we didn't want a loaded gun around, you know, and then when we got—before we got all the stuff back to the house I said to her let's put that gun down in that storage room because, you know, I didn't particularly want it around the house and my little two girls—I have two little girls that came up and lived with us in the summer and stuff and I didn't want the thing around and uh-I put it in a sack—a Safeway sack…

(Police interview transcript, Nov. 7, 1975, p. 44.)

Merrilyn [Mimi] Forrest also spoke about the .38 revolver in the camper that belonged to Alga and her:

MF:… I had to have something to bargain with, see, he [Alga] had a lot of stereo equipment in our trailer. Well, I got down there and Jerry was down there, and we borrowed a van from my brother, we were going to go down and get that stereo equipment and come back up, but when we go down there—this sounds terrible! —when we got down there we took the camper because it was there and it was in my name.

Interviewer: Was he [Alga] there when you took it?

MF: He was sleeping in the trailer.

I: Did he know you took it?

MF: No, not until the next morning when I called him. That's how I got the gun. It was in the camper.

I: Well—so you took off with Jerry in the camper?

MF: No, Jerry drove the camper and I drove the van.

I: Okay, and the gun was in the back of the camper?

MF: Yeah.

I: Okay, and what did you do with the stuff that you had brought out then?

MF: Cleaned it out, kept all the important stuff, dumped the rest and then eventually I gave him the camper back and put all the clothing in that and kept the gun because we were afraid to give the gun back to him.

I: What'd you do with the gun then?

MF: Okay, Jerry put it upstairs in the top closet in the apartment. We live in a very, very, very, very bad part of town—there's drugs. They're always asking on the street whether you want to buy drugs—I want to explain this because uh, it's just a bad, you can't go out at night—

I: Did your husband have any bullets with the gun?

MF: Yeah, but Jerry threw 'em right away—

I: So you kept the gun without any bullets?

MF: Yeah.

I: And kept an empty revolver in the apartment?

MF: Yeah, it wasn't for protection.

I: Oh, I see—

MF: It was just—we couldn't give it back, but we couldn't get rid of it, you know.

I: Did you see Jerry throw the bullets away?

MF: Yeah.

I: Where did he throw them?

MF: I don't remember—I just remember him taking the bullets out and throwing them—and I can't remember where it was, but I remember seeing him do it—absolutely—and it wasn't full of bullets, but only like four in it or something like that, I can't remember but I don't think it was full.

I: Were there any bullets in the camper, you know, boxes of shells?

MF: No—no, 'cause I remember this—my father-in-law gave the gun to my husband, but only gave him four bullets…

I: Did your husband ever buy any shells?

MF: No—he had no need to use it, you know,…so Jerry put it up in the closet and then the girls came, his girls came for the whole summer. He didn't want the gun in the house, I don't know why, there were no bullets in it, but the girls were there and he's very protective of his little girls, you know, he loves them, and so he put it downstairs in the storage room.

I: Was it in the basement of the house?

MF:…there's an alley underneath our apartment that's accessible to anyone and everyone where there are storage sheds on each side with just those hasp locks and a small lock in it and the lock that Jerry had, it was very cheap—in fact my father was amazed at why we had such a cheap lock on it, but we didn't have anything of importance in there—nothing—we just threw all our junk stuff down there and the gun.

    I: Well, when the girls came you put the gun down in the locker?

    MF: Yeah, it was the week prior to June 2nd when we came out here.

    (Police interview transcript, Nov. 7, 1975, pp. 12-13 ff.)

2. Family Visit

Merrilyn Forest described their summer, 1975 visit to her future in-laws:

    Interviewer: The four of you [Jerry, his daughters, and Merrilyn] came back to Iowa?

    MF: Uh huh.

    I: How did you get back here?

    MF: Jerry's dad paid for the tickets for the… plane flight.

    I: And how long did you stay in Iowa at that time?

    MF: I stayed a week.

    I: How long did Jerry stay?

    MF: He stayed about three weeks.

    I: And you flew back to Berkeley?

    MF: Yeah.

    I: And did he stay with his two girls here? [at the Homeplace]

    MF: No—he stayed a few more days, and he took his girls to Rebecca's [his estranged wife] parents' house [in Iowa] because they wanted the girls to visit for a couple of weeks. And he left them off, then Jerry went to Renato [Renato Balestra, his friend from Brazil from Peace Corps days] house for the rest of the time. I think he flew home from there [Renato's house] after he picked up the girls.

    I: Flew home?

    MF: Uh huh.

    I: What was his purpose for coming out in the first place?

    MF: His father was starting chemotherapy treatments and Jerry was afraid his father was going to die, you know—that's the impression he got on the phone, and his dad said come out, I want to see the girls before I die, or I get so bad that I can't talk to them or relate to them so that's why we came out.

    (Interview transcript, November 7, pp. 15-16.)

George Colthurst, Jorjean's father, also spoke of that family meeting in May.

    "Jerry wanted right back into farming, right now. In Jorjean's letter [to her father and mother] and Les just simply told him, 'No sir we tried that once.

And it didn't work. Either you were in town, or asleep when dad and I were doing the work, and we're not going to do it again.".... Then he went to his dad, and Wayne Mark himself told him, we were out riding around in a car, looking at the crops, and Wayne told him, he said, 'I just told him, it's not fair to Les and Jorjean. They went way in debt. And borrowed a lot of money, and they coulda lost their shirt, could lost it all, went under, but... fortunately they hit some good years, and some good grain prices, and they got their feet on the ground, and they're goin'. And [Wayne said to Jerry] 'I subsidized you from the day you were born. And you're educated, you can make a living, now get out and go to work.' Wayne himself told me that." (George and Margaret Colthurst interview, July 10, 1980, p. 13)

"...the problem was Jerry came back [in May] and he could see that Les was getting more and more control. Of the family operation. And Wayne [father] was putting more and more responsibility on Les. Now he was grooming him [Les] in to the real estate business as well. Going to take that over. And Jerry couldn't stand this. He wanted right back in without a dime. In the farming. And of course when Wayne told Jerry no, and Wayne wouldn't have told me this, but Les did, he said Jerry said to his dad, 'Old man, next time I come back here, it'll be to piss on your grave.' That came out at the trial." (George and Margaret Colthurst interview, July 10, 1980, p. 15)

Dorothy Mark also spoke of the argument in the family over the care of Tom:

"All right, now, Tom is our third son. Tom is a very talented young man. He's a perfectionist. He...he can't live with himself. He has had trouble, uh, he has good periods and bad periods in his life and, uh, he—he wasn't doing well. He has rather a, I cannot say the word, schizophrenic tendencies. He gets very paranoid, too. Uh, right now he is fine—he's on his way back again. But, about what should be done for Tom. And the disagreement came over what should be done for Tom, with two different points of view: Jerry felt we should go... Les and Wayne and Jerry were the ones that were yelling about it—were discussing it. Uh, Jerry's point of view was that we should do everything possible—and, and they were talking to their father because their father more or less controlled the money in our family... in some ways he was very generous, some ways he was not, But he handled the say so. Jerry was trying to convince him that he should go all out, that Tom maybe should be sent to Menningers in Kansas... And we should go all out to cure this. Les had the feeling that there was no cure and that what we should do is find a place where Tom would be kept happy and clean and well-fed and well taken care of, but we should not go throwing out money after uh… "

(Dorothy Mark Interview, July 14, 1980, pp. 1-2.

Mimi spoke of one other issue that bothered Jerry his entire adult life, caused by his father: a physical injury to his tailbone.

Interviewer: What's Jerry's background, what happened there?

M: Oh gosh, what did happen? His father he hit him when he was a kid, very hard—and broke his tailbone—and ever since then he's had problems—

I: Does walking bother him, or… ?

M: Oh, it's the way he sits—he doesn't sit right because he has a tailbone sticking out right on his—and it's red and it's a big bump, you know—so he sits wrong so it's a matter of he's lifted too much and he sits wrong… "

(Police interview transcript, Nov. 7, p. 42)

3. Planning

During her November 7 interview with detectives, Merrilyn Forrest remembered when Jerry bought the Honda 450 motorcycle; before that he had only owned a small 100cc motorbike.

Interviewer: When did Jerry get the other motorbike [Honda 450]?

Merrilyn: Not too long ago—about three weeks before he left on this trip.

I: Where did he get the money to pay for it?

M: Father—

I: Wayne?

M: Yeah, he borrowed some money from Wayne and he was supposed to buy a car. Well, I bought the car and he bought the motorcycle with the money.

I: How long has he been planning this trip?

M: Well, he talked to me a lot about it and we had been having some real bad difficulties between us about Rebecca and about my divorce and he—just never got to go and then finally I told him to go and I'd give him the money to go.

I: How much did you give him?

M: A hundred dollars—but he spent some of that before he left so I guess he left with about seventy dollars.

I: What'd he spend it on?

M: Well, he had some money left over and he bought a suit, you know, a motorcycle suit—it's called Belfast. [Belstaff] This consisted of pants that were large so he could get a lot of clothes underneath and a covering top that zipped, I think.

I: What color is it?

M: Black, perfectly black.

I: What else did he buy?

M: A white helmet—white with black stripe on it and…a radio. I guess he never used it [on the trip] 'cause I thought he might have heard about it on the radio, but he said he didn't listen to it.

I: How long had he been talking about this trip?

M: About a couple of months.

I: Anyone else beside yourself know he was going to take a trip?

M: No, it wasn't planned—it was more like, I'd like to do this, you know.

I: Did Rebecca know?

M: No—because all of a sudden it came up, you know, that he was going to go. We had talked about it a little bit, but not like specifically—he just said I'd like to go on a trip sometime, I'd like to feel, you know, the freedom…

I: And he bought the bike especially for this trip?

M: No, he bought it for transportation.

I: OK, [you mentioned] the Sunday before Halloween is when he decided…

M: Yeah, in the car.

I: What kind of preparations was made through the week?

M: I gave him the hundred dollars on 10-28. He worked on the motorcycle a bit, thought that something was wrong with the timing. And he had been working on it prior to that trying to get it going good, and he was having a good time…

I: Do you recall the date that Jerry received the money that Wayne sent, the money that he used to buy the motorcycle?

M: (whispering) I have no idea. I have no idea.

I: Did he say where he was going to ride to?

M: We talked about it the night before he left and he said he was gonna go down to southern California to the desert, and that's where he started off and—oh, gosh—he was having such a good time—I never saw him when he called me so happy as on that trip. It made him feel so independent, you know. (Police interview transcript, Nov. 7, pp. 17-19.)

Jerry bought a Honda 450 on October 3, 1975. Steve Sweeney, a Berkeley resident sold it, according to his testimony during the trial:

Dutton: Would you indicate when it was sold and how you went about the sale of that motorcycle?

Sweeney: Well, I ran an ad in the Oakland Tribune on the 2nd of October, and I got a phone call from Jerry Mark, and he came over and looked at the bike and bought it... the following day.

D: Do you see him in the courtroom today?

S: Yes, I do.

D: And would you point him out to the jury?

S: That gentleman right there.

...

D: Did you have any conversation with the Defendant...?

S: Well, I just noticed it [the Iowa license plate on his small Honda] and... he said he was from Iowa. That was really the extent of it.

(Trial Transcripts, Vol. 7, pp. 1632-3.)

4. Ammunition

During the trial, David Dutton questioned Jack Makendonski about selling a box of .38 Long Colt cartridges to Jerry Mark.

Dutton: Mr. Makendonski, did you, in the year 1975, sell a box of .38 Long Winchester Western ammunition to one Jerry Allen Mark?

Makendonski: Yes, I did.

D: Will you tell the jury on what date your records show that you sold that box of ammunition to Jerry Allen Mark?

M:...[the cash register roll] shows the 20th of October, 1975.

D:...what procedure is followed and what kind of information is taken to record that sale? [Besides the cash register roll]

M:...we are required to record the name of the individual and also an identification number—social security number or driver's license is usually what is used. And this has to be produced, and we record it.

D: I want to hand you what has been marked by the [Court] Reporter as State's Exhibit 203, and ask you to look at it and tell us what it is.

M: This is the same book that was attached to the cash register at that time.

... The first entry is November 8, 1974, and the last entry is November 8, 1975:

D: And do you find in that book any indication that Jerry Allen Mark purchased a box of .38 Long Colt Ammunition?

M: Yes, I do.

D: And in whose handwriting is that information?

M: It's in my handwriting.

D:... And is that an accurate and a complete record of ammunition sales that you have been involved in as a partner and also a salesman for Ken's Sport Shop?

M: Yes, it is.

D:...And what information is contained in that portion of the book, State's Exhibit 203? Would you just read it to the jury, please?

M: ".38 Long Colt, Jerry Allen Mark, [SS #], Iowa driver's license."

D:...Was there anything about the fact that it was an Iowa driver's license that caught your attention?

M: Yes, there was. I was born in Waterloo, Iowa and I had a conversation with the individual concerning that.

D: Do you remember... approximately what that discussion was?

M: Well, I always made it a point to try to be friendly to everybody that comes in, especially somebody new.

D: When you say "somebody new," had you ever seen this person before?

M: No, I hadn't.

D: And you say you make it a habit to try to be friendly?

M: Right. And seeing it was an Iowa driver's license, it gave me a subject to discuss while I was taking care of the sale itself.

D: And what, if anything, do you recall about the responses of the purchaser?

M: I know the individual was polite, and at least answered my questions.

D:...how many boxes of .38 Long Colt ammunition [did you have] in your store at the time this person came in and purchased that box?

M: At the most, we had three boxes, because that is all we have a record of receiving in the entire existence of the business.

D:...When the [BCI] investigators came to your store some time in early November, what was done with the remaining boxes of ammunition of the .38 Long Colt variety?

M: We had two boxes. They purchased one, and that was November 8, 1975. Then after that, they purchased the last box which we had in stock, and that would be recorded in the book that's presently at the store. [After November 8].

(Trial Transcript, Book XX, pp. 790-800.)

The ammunition itself was extremely unusual; as noted above Makendonski testified that he rarely had seen a box of .38 Long Colt cartridges, much less sold them. Don McCollister, a supervisor at Winchester-Western, who made the ammunition, offered the following testimony about its rarity:

Dutton: You said that your total production of pistol and rifle ammunition was 246 million loaded rounds? [in 1975]

McCollister: That's right.

D: Does Winchester Western produce a caliber of ammunition called .38 Long Colt?

M: Yes, sir.

D: And what percentage of the total production of ammunition is represented by .38 Long Colt, in referring specifically to the year 1975?

M: In 1975, we produced 259,000 loaded rounds, which is about 1% of our total pistol-revolver production.

D: All right.

M: This is a small seller, so to speak. It's not used very much. We don't have but a few sales for this item.

[Trial Transcript, Book III, p. 687]

5. Ride to Iowa

Here are letters that crossed in the mail between Jerry and Les while Jerry was riding to Iowa. Jerry wrote his on Oct. 27, the day before he left Berkeley, and Les wrote to Jerry the next day, responding to a request that Jerry had made on the phone to Jorjean a few days before.

October 27, 1975. [postmarked Oct. 28]

Dear Les,

Sorry I missed talking to you the other evening, but it was good to visit with Jorjean. I should have written sooner, as by waiting I probably left you up in the air a little concerning the job reference which I discussed with Jorjean. [on the telephone the week before]

However, the day after I called I got a form letter from the employment office concerned, saying they had hired someone else. So I put off writing since the urgency concerning that job application was gone.

Anyway, what I would appreciate being able to do, is to list in the "previous employment" section of future job applications that I farmed with you as a general partner during the 1973 and 1974 crop years, or from March of 1973 to December of 1974. This would enable me to present a much more stable and responsible employment history than I am otherwise able to do, and that would be most helpful in the job market. I believe I am generally informed enough about your operation to respond to questions concerning such hypothetical employment in an adequate manner during job interviews, so it would be a low-risk falsehood in the circumstances. You could respond to any inquiries made by my prospective employers based upon your actual operation, modifying it only to the extent to pretend that we were general operating partners. If this is agreeable to you I would appreciate it greatly.

I will say I made about $1000 a month or $10,000 for the year (ten months) in 1973, and that 1974 was better so I made $1250/month or $15,000 for the second year.

I'll also say I sold out my interest in the machinery and grain at the end of 1974, and relocated here to California, due to my marital problems and divorce, and my desire to start over fresh and also be near the kids here in California.

Otherwise than this 1973-4 period my job and education history is not too bad, so I am not misrepresenting anything else to any significant extent. But this part really needs cleaning up, to get a good job.

Mimi and I bought a used VW Superbeatle [sic] from a 75-year-old lady with only 23,000 miles of town driving on it, so it is in great condition. I've got some good dress clothes now, and also last week made the ultimate sacrifice of shaving, so now I hope to have better luck on the job market.

If I don't get a good job in the next month or 2, I'll probably have to get a mediocre temporary job to tide me over and build the savings back up, before trying again for a good job. But I am optimistic that I can present myself well enough to land a good job soon.

Les, I don't want to put you in a situation you don't agree with or don't want to do, so I urge you to let me know right away if you don't want me to list you in the manner I outlined above as a past job reference. I could work out something else in that case.

I hope the harvest is going great and that your family is fine. Drop me a line sometime when you have time, later this winter.

Best regards,

Jerry

From Les to Jerry:

October 28, 1975 [postmarked Oct. 29]

Dear Jerry:

I'm sorry I haven't answered sooner. Glad to hear from you and I too hope we can stay in close touch. I'm glad your back is improving. I have always thought I had a strong back but this moving that that I've done the last two months really put me in pain. So I can now honestly say that I have at least some idea of what you have been living with and I hope you do whatever you must in the way work, hobbies, lifestyle or operations, if need be, to take care of yourself.

I am glad to hear that you and Mimi are living happily together. Mimi seems like a nice gal. The short time we were together and under the circumstances of your Iowa visit were very poor conditions to get to know anyone. But I trust in the future we can meet in a more pleasurable atmosphere. Please say hello to her from me.

My family is just great! Jorjean has been very busy taking care of all of us, moving then trying to get settled, feeding the Renner crew and the usual household work.

Julie is growing up and is such a sweet little girl. (I hope you don't mind if I brag a little—it's all true of course!!!) Julie was sick recently with a bladder infection but will soon be back to normal. Jeff is full of the devil—always on the go with an independent mind of his own. I love all of them and would be lost without them.

The harvest here is moving right along. Hope to be done by Nov. 8th or 10th. Have done a lot of fieldwork and hope to do more. Have a chance to rent another farm west of C.F. Bill and Leo and Dad have bought it. I am planning on getting my real estate license this winter as I am already doing some work for them.

Moving into this house was a major undertaking in itself. We are very happy to be here now while we are young enough to put his house back in shape and while our children are growing up. Mother and Dad are in a beautiful house in Turkey Foot. They'll both live long enough to fall in love with it and some day moving from it will be a hard thing for them to do. The yard isn't that much smaller than what Dad had to care of before. It has grapes, apple trees, asparagus plants, raspberries, not just one of a kind but rows of them of different types. Mother is at home already. It is such a good deal for her—easier to care, new, decorated. She will also enjoy the change to have some woman companionship.

I am now about to stop writing and will go to bed; I think I'll mail this to you as it is and write more later—rather than laying it on my desk until it is completed.

As far as Tom is concerned I am very pleased that you are concerned and are willing to help by means of beefing up a trust if need be. I am sure you, Dick, and I can take care of everything. I do feel that I am going to have to continue to help him. Today I had Tom sign a Power of Attorney to me. I am handling a house closing for him Friday on an old deal Dad set up for him in 1969. I am also going to sell his car as he is not able to keep it running and last week was the 4th time I've gotten it out of storage after being towed in. Each time the same problem—no gas. It runs out. Tom walks away. The cops ticket it and then have it towed. Pass along any ideas you have. Sorry this letter is such a mess.

Love, Les.

Jerry Mark's story about his motorcycle ride to Iowa remained essentially the same in two interviews. The first, to Detective Edwin Newman in South Lake Tahoe occurred on Monday, November 3rd, when Newman interviewed both Mark and Merrilyn Forrest and the second, four days later on November 7 by detectives in Cedar Falls. Both interviews reveal Jerry's alibi story up to late Saturday morning, November 1st, when he says he left western Nebraska near Chappell and started back to California. They are similar enough that I offer only the November 3rd version.

Newman: About what time did you leave? [Berkeley, on Wednesday, Oct. 29]

Jerry Mark: I think it was around 9:00 in the morning.

N: Where were you headed to?

JM: Uh, I headed down—my original plan was to spend about three or three and a half days down in the Mojave Desert, and uh, so I headed down—uh, I didn't want to drive on the freeways so about—about half way down there or a little less than half than half I drove on it, there's a mountain road that's—that's between Highway 101 and Highway 5 and then—uh—I didn't make real good time at first, you know. My backpack—I mean my, this stuff that you pack on the motorcycle—this was the first time I'd ever done this.

N: I see.

JM: And I wasn't too well organized, you know, and uh, I almost lost my sleeping bag and stuff—it just too a long time at first, I had to stop every little bit and reorganize things and I called Mimi about supper time.

N: Do you remember the name of the town?

MF: Coalinga.

JM: Yeah, from that little town of Coalinga, right, which is sort of,... between these two highways in there and I'd just come down a mountain drive when I—to get to Coalinga and then from Coalinga I think the road went over to Highway—it's close to Bakersfield because, you know, I was in Bakersfield and,...

N: This would have been the night of the 29th?

JM: Right.

N: Where did you stay that night?

JM: Well, then I drove real light because I—things started working out good on the motorcycle and I stayed—and I drove—I drove the freeway too which I made good time on—

N: Uh huh.

JM: And I drove on to Barstow—the town right on the area of the Mojave Desert. And I stayed—I camped outside of town.

N: Did you stay in a designated campground?

JM: No, I just pulled off the side of the road and slept in a –oh, kinda like a little grassy driveway, you know.

N: Do you know what highway that was?

JM: Uh-whatever—whatever that highway is—

N: That goes from Los Angeles to Las Vegas?

JM: Uh—that main highway runs into Barstow—uh, it was pretty late.

N: What time was it?

JM: I think I bedded in about 3:00 AM.

N: Okay.

JM: Yeah, it was a long—you know it was a long day—

N: What time did you get up?

JM: I was on the road around 6:00.

N: 6:00 AM?

JM: Yeah, really—what happened was in this little—there was really, uh, I don't know, it was a beautiful thing because there was a little bird chirping right by my sleeping bag and the little bird couldn't have been more than just a few feet from me—it was a weird experience, but that woke me up and I felt real good and it was a beautiful day—and uh so—I—you know—I was really on a carefree—having a lark, you know?

N: Where did you go from there, from Barstow?

JM: I headed over—this is where I changed my plans because… my first idea was to just kind of bum it in that locality 'cause I thought it would be nice warm place to bum around.

N: Had you ever been there before?

JM: Never. I'd been through the Imperial Valley—but the thing is I wanted to just have some time to myself but I enjoyed the machine so much—you know, this motorcycle.

N: Uh huh.

JM: And the last part of the drive I had done so good, you know, that I just wanted to drive, so I—uh—you know—I had noticed the signs to Las Vegas so I just…

N: You went through Las Vegas?

JM: No, no, I drove right through—I passed through there fairly easily and uh, and I—I—you know I got on this Interstate Highway going north and I headed up north and ended up spending the night—well, I called Mimi again when she got off work that night.

MF: Yeah, it was about 9:00.

JM: Was it that late?

MF: Yeah.

JM: Do you remember the town?

MF: You said you were outside Provo or you were going to Provo, Utah.

JM: Yeah—I was—I was somewhere in there—

N: Okay so that would have been around 9:30.

JM: Yeah but I didn't spend the night. I got up [that night] to Salt Lake City.

N: Every time that you called did you call collect?

JM: I just made a station call—just paid for my calls—I did at first, now I ran out of money at the end of the trip so I called collect yesterday.

N: So on the night of the 30th where did you spend the night?

JM: East of Salt Lake City—this night it snowed—this is where I really made the stupid mistake—which caused all the grief because my original plan was I told Mimi Thursday night was I just wanted to go up to the Salt Lake area and this was the next day and then I'd come half way home [starting Friday] and she said, well, you're having such a good time when don't you go, but I felt guilty about maybe missing that Saturday night party and I'm having a lot of fun goofing around...

N: What town or city were you close to that night?

JM: I really don't know—it was very late and I was totally wiped out.

N: But it was in the Utah area?

JM: I'm not sure whether it was—I think I was—I—I—it was in the vicinity of the border between the states but whether or not I was still in Utah or across I don't remember.

N: Interstate 80? Somewhere?

JM: Right, 'cause it started snowing and I'd kinda gotten settled there and I slept a little bit fitfully and I woke up and it was lightly snowing.

N: I see.

JM: And I thought I'd better find out what's going on and I went up to the first truck stop and got a cup of coffee and got warmed up and stuff and listened to the talk—and they said it was snowing back in Utah and the roads were closed and the snow was coming this way—

N: Uh huh, do you know what café that was or what area that was in?

JM: Uh—

N: The time of day or night?

JM: Well, that was—uh—I—I don't know the café, but I –I mean I might be able to—I could maybe go and retrace it or something if—if

N: It was on Interstate 80?

JM: Yeah.

N: Do you know what time it was?

JM: Right—I think it was around 5:00 probably.

N: 5:00 in the morning?

JM: Yeah—in that—in that…

N: What time had you gone to bed…?

JM: Probably around 3:30 or 4:00 or something—

N: So in other words you only stayed in bed for about a half an hour or so?

JM: That time, yeah—uh—maybe an hour, you know, to… this was—this was the same day of the, you know, the grueling second day, you know, and I got carried away and I'd over-extended on my—and ah—

N: After leaving the café where did you go?

JM: Well, then I should have holed up there but uh—I went on up to you know on up the—further west—east, I mean, further into the mountains and it was a dumb thing, but… I was tired and irrational and run down and I felt like—oh, my God, what if I get caught in the snow and can't get back for this party, you know, and what's Mimi gonna think 'cause I told her that night earlier I was gonna be back…I'd kinda gotten myself into a jam, you know, and uh…

N: You went eastbound, further up?

JM: East—towards uh—I think the next town is uh—

N: And that was on Interstate 80?

JM: Right—the next town is uh—Rawlins, Wyoming—and I wore myself out trying to talk to what the other drivers were saying…

N: How far did you go that day, being the 31st, Friday?

JM: I went all the way that day to Chappell, Nebraska—I tried to get ahold of Mimi but she went out with some friends and I couldn't get her, but I had a divorce hearing today [Monday] and so I had to get home Sunday evening…

N: Where did you end up staying?

JM: This time I stayed at a rest area right on Interstate 80 at a designated—

N: Here's a map here, Jerry—

JM: It's Chappell or Chapel or something like this out in the western panhandle.

N: Okay, so this was the night of the 30th, or the 31st—Friday night?

JM: This was the third night—Friday night.

(Police interview transcript, November 3rd, pp. 1-8.)

6. The Marks' Halloween

Les and Jorjean spent their late afternoon and early evening on Halloween with Dennis and Barbara Wulf, who described it this way:

Dutton: When did you make contact with the family that night?

Wulf: They came to our house between 8:15 and 8:30 that night.

D: And all four of them were present?

W: Yes.

D: What did you do when they came to your house?

W: We just sat and talked. They just stopped by and they were there for about an hour.

D: Were the children at all excited about Halloween or doing tricks or treats?

W: We gave them Halloween candy, but they weren't dressed up for Halloween.

D: They weren't. Were they disappointed, in talking about that at all?

W: Well, earlier that might when I had talked to Jorjean on the phone, she had said that Julie was mad because they weren't going to get to go trick-or-treating, so that's why I said why don't you come in and go to our house.

D: And you gave them some candy?

W: Yeah.

D: All right. When did they leave your house on that evening?

W: Probably about between 9:15 and 9:30.

D: And that's the last you ever saw of them?

W: Yes.

(Trial transcript, Book I, p. 116.)

Dorothy Mark explained her visit to Les and his family that night after Les and Jorjean returned from the Wulfs:

When I was down there that night, I said to Julie, "Are you going trick-or-treating?" And she said, "No, we're going to have our own little party here." And I said, "What are you going to do?" And she said, "Well, daddy's gonna come in before I have to go to bed and Mother's made chocolate pudding, and we're going to have our own Halloween party here." When I opened the dishwasher [the next afternoon, after the murders] the dishes were in there from the chocolate pudding. And they had had some sort of a red drink, Kook-Aid or something. The dishes were not washed.

I: And Victor had been there, about 10:00?

DM: Victor was there, yet, at 1:00. Victor left about 1:00. Les went in from doing the corn about 12:30 because he was going to up and over at the dryer at 6:00 [the next morning]. And Vic stayed to unload the corn [that night].
(Dorothy Mark interview transcript, July 14, 1980, p. 40.)

Autopsy evidence revealed that Jorjean had been penetrated anally that night, or "sodomized" to use the negative term. There were also condoms on the bedroom floor and a Vaseline jar nearby. For a time, Jerry wanted to show that Jorjean may have been raped by the intruder, but condoms and petroleum jelly would not support that assertion. Both the prosecution and the defense agreed that probably the young couple had enjoyed anal intercourse that night, and the defense gave up pursuing DNA evidence testing relating to this potential issue.

7. Intruder

For the jury, David Dutton described what he thought must have happened in the homeplace that night, given the physical evidence at the scene:

"The Defendant entered the house, using a key that had hung near the back door on a nail for as long as the Mark family had been part of that household. It's what many, many families do, because everybody doesn't carry a key or doesn't have one all the time. And so on the back porch, right on the side of one of the windows, there was a key hanging on a nail.

The Defendant entered the house. Of course, it's difficult to know what actually happened first, when it happened, but the evidence will show that in the basement by the furnace, there were cigarette butts, Marlboro cigarettes, that were stamped out on the floor. And the Defendant smokes Marlboro cigarettes. And in checking the saliva on the filter of that cigarette, it was determined that whoever smoked it had Type O blood and was a secreter. Many people have Type O blood and are secreters, and so does the Defendant.

The evidence will show that some time after the children were in bed and some time after Les and Jorjean got into their bed in the downstairs bedroom—the children were in the two upstairs bedrooms—the Defendant entered the bedroom and stood at the foot of the bed, and that Les and Jorjean woke up. They saw him. There was a struggle, an attempt to disarm the Defendant. The gun went off, fired the first shot into the floor. The next shot went between Les and Jorjean, grazing her side. Les and Jorjean were made to get off the bed, kneel on the floor, holding pillows in front of them, and then they were both shot.

Les was shot twice in the back of the head, once immediately in the back and once over the left ear. He was also shot through the stomach, and he was also shot twice, once through each jaw.

Jorjean was shot once right in the middle of the back, severing her spine and traveling through her heart. She was also shot twice in the back of the head, with both bullets entering exactly the same hole.

Both of them were killed in that manner in the bedroom, with ten shots, ten rounds of .38 Long ammunition killing them in that bedroom.

The two children were upstairs. There is some evidence that Julie, the little girl, the five-year-old, woke up during the noise that was being made. There was a pillow from her bed near the door leading out of that bedroom. She was in bed when she was killed. There was a bullet in her brain and there was a bullet in her heart. There was, on the floor of that bedroom near the dresser, a Marlboro cigarette that had been stamped out, with an O-Type blood indication from the saliva on the cigarette filter.

The little boy's room was across the hall. He was killed in exactly the same way, with a bullet in the brain and a bullet in the heart.

After the inhabitants of that house were killed, the Defendant went down and he did several things that are rather tell-tale: first of all, he smashed the face or the glass of the door of the grandfather clock; then went to the basement and turned off all of the electricity, turned off all the circuit breakers. And in the house, the clock that Leslie had set to go off at 4:30 to wake him up so that he could start work the next morning, went off at 3:05 A.M., which would indicate that that was the time that the power was turned off at the house by the killer.

The Defendant then left by the back door, closed it and locked it. He took a potted plant from the back porch, from one of the tables, and he threw it through the window. He had already pulled out the drawers in several of the desks in the house to make it appear that someone had broken in to ransack the house, but nothing was missing. The potted plant through the window was a way to cover up what was the real motive of the person involved." (Trial transcript, Book I, pp. 80-83.)

8. Discovery

Dorothy Mark described what happened when she and Clark Renner discovered the bodies:

DM: Could I start back a little while and tell Clark's story?

Interviewer: Sure.

DM: He got up and had breakfast maybe 4:30. He got up very early. He and Les had an agreement that Les would be over at the [Renner's] dryer, which is three or four miles over here on [Highway] 218 at 6:00. Les had gone in the house about 12:30 and Victor had stayed to finish unloading.... The story that he told me, and he told it over and over again to whoever would listen that morning, is that he got up and he came down and just drove through the yard at, around 4:30 in the morning.

I: Through Les's yard.

DM:... just to see if they got the corn unloaded. Then he went over the dryer and he did some work....He tried to call Les in there. And so, he came back again—the trucks that held the corn were backed into the shed. That's all he saw the first time. He came back the second time and went out to the elevator which was out back of the pole building, to, I don't know, to walk, he went out there. And then he came and checked the trucks again... without going into the house.

I: And this is about what time?

DM: About six. Les had not got over there. He [Clark Renner] had some work to do on the... dryer and he did the work and they kept an old davenport in there and he thought Les would be coming any time and he just sat down on the davenport and went to sleep.... And then he came back to [Les's] the house and told us "I was just gonna go up and I was gonna run in the house yelling good and loud and I was gonna holler at Les about laying in bed with his wife, instead of getting up and doing the work."

And he went up to the house and he saw the broken window in a door. You had to go in the south side of the house at that time—you went in through a screen door into a little tiny porch, and our door had a great big window—the whole top of it was glass. And that was broken. Someone had picked a plant up and thrown in from the outside in, and the plant was an asparagus fern and the plant lay broken in there. And she [Jorjean] had had her plants—there was a worktable out on this little porch and she had some of her plants there. And he [Clark Renner] said "Somebody's come up here." He did not go in...had I been at this house and saw that, I would have gone in to help.

I: He didn't even try to go in?

DM: He didn't go in. He came up and he met me at the door. I was getting breakfast, Wayne was in his office then, probably on the telephone. Uh, because he was, well, he never did lose his mind, he lost his ability to talk and to see, and somewhat to walk. Mostly to walk. But, Clark said, "Well, now there's something awful wrong down there… have you, Wayne talked to Les yet this morning?" And no, he [Wayne] hadn't.

I: Wayne had tried to call?

DM: Wayne had tried. And Clark said, "Well, I don't get an answer, and I tried him from the pickup and I've tried him from the dryer." Clark has a telephone in his pickup. And he says, "There's something wrong, there's been somebody down there doing Halloween damage or something because the window is broken in the door. And I had asked him when he came in, if he didn't want a cup of coffee because he always had coffee with us. No, he didn't.

I: Did you have a bad feeling at that point?

DM: No!

I: You just thought that, what did you suspect? Anything?

DM: I just thought Renner'd been drinking.

I: Uh huh. OK.

DM: Thought Renner had a hangover, maybe…I said to him, "What do you want me to do? Do you want me to go down and see what's wrong down there?"

And, yes. And Wayne—I couldn't leave Wayne, or I didn't want to leave Wayne. And of course if something happened on the farm he wanted to be there. And so we go down and go in and I'm first, here's this door broken.

I: Did you have any trouble getting the door open?

A: I reached in… and unlocked it.

I:… Clark testified in the trial he couldn't get it open…

DM: The key hung right up there. Everybody in the country knew that! All the kids—college friends—would come. I would get up in the morning and there would be kids who had come in and open up the house and gone to bed, down for breakfast. It's OK. I didn't care. Everybody knew and I don't know how many people had keys. I know that all our children had keys and I know that some of their friends had keys and it's just one of those old doors…

I: So it was just a skeleton key?

DM: No, it was a key, it was lock key that went into the knob. But I reached in the broken door and unlocked the door and went in and I called to them right away, and they didn't… I didn't get any answer. So I went into the bedrooms, still yelling…

I: Were you bothered then? Did it cross your mind that you might find them dead?

DM: Midwest, middle-class, Midwest farm people—nothing happens like that! Nothing crossed my mind. I just went calling to them. I'm sure that I began to know that was wrong. Well, I got to the bedroom door—it opens into the bedroom. And I knocked and knocked on it and yelled and nobody answered so I opened the door to go on and Les's body was against the door holding it shut. And I could only get it open about this far but I could, I got my head and one shoulder in.

I: Did you know that it was Les or you thought maybe it was furniture or something?

DM: Just something was against the door. However, I could see Jorjean right away. And Jorjean was lying on an angle toward—with her head toward the window, face down. She had on a little light blue baby-doll nightie, and I could see the bullet. I only saw one bullet hole in Jorjean—through the back of her nightie. And then I looked. And now all I saw of Les was an arm thrown up. Les had on perhaps his shorts, perhaps shorty pajamas—I don't know—that's all I could see.

Well of course I ran right away too, I said to Clark who was behind me—said to him, "think they're dead, they've been shot." I couldn't see that Les had been shot, but I knew that nobody would shoot Jorjean. They'd have to kill Les first.

And, so, I went and ran to the telephone and phone book, and our uh, dining room there, what they were using for the dining room is an inside room and it is dark. We use a light all the time. And I said to Clark, "Go downstairs and turn the circuit breaker on." And he started down the stairs and he said "Dorothy, maybe the kids, what about the kids? Maybe we better go see about the kids."

So I dropped the telephone... I went tearing through the rest of the house and up the front stairs. The children slept in the front bedrooms. And went in to see Julie and she was in bed lying on her back with a, a hole in her chest, a bullet wound. And with her, one in her head and her face just peppered with blue marks, or purplish marks! I didn't know what those were. And after we got the police called Clark went to the phone and called his wife and said to here, "Get down here quick, Dorothy needs you." She thought Les or Wayne had got caught in the elevator that was unloading the corn. She came down and sat with us. And so I told her about—she didn't go to look at the children, but I told her and she told me those were powder marks. You know, but I didn't know that.

Q: And then you went to Jeff's room.

DM: And then we went to Jeff's room and Jeff was laying in his cradle with his head towards the middle of the room and he had the, almost the very same except I don't know if it was same side of his head. No powder burns on him… .Everybody believes that Julie heard the shots downstairs, and she was out of bed. Because her pillow was on the floor. Uh, I do not remember seeing her pillow on the floor.

… So then we went back downstairs and Clark couldn't find the circuit breakers and I went down and turned it on and I came and called the police. (Dorothy Mark Interview, July 14, 1980, transcript, pp. 9-12)

Dorothy also described her first reaction:

When they asked "How did you find Mrs. Mark? Well, she was hysterical."

Well, I'm not an hysterical person. They asked Clark how did I act, and he said I screamed. Well, I didn't scream. I went, Aaaww, Clark, look at this!" I didn't scream and I'm not hysterical, though maybe I will be."

(Dorothy Mark interview transcript, July 14, 1980, p. 14)

9. Investigating Begins

This chapter arose from several extended conversations with both David Dutton and Tom Ruxlow, a recent interview (2010) with David Correll, and newspaper accounts. Both the Cedar Falls *Record* and Waterloo *Courier* carried detailed stories about the days immediately following the murders. This excerpt appeared in the *Courier* on Sunday, Nov. 2nd.

The bodies were discovered about 8:00 AM by a neighboring farmer, Clark Renner, and Mark's mother, Mrs. Wayne Mark, who lives in the area. She summoned sheriff's deputies.

The area was cordoned off and deputies began an exhaustive search for clues in the house surrounding areas outside.

Shortly after noon, the bodies of the murder victims were taken to St. Francis Hospital for examination by County Deputy Medical Examiner Dr. Edward Ceilly.

For a time, authorities considered a murder-suicide theory but that theory was dismissed after investigators failed to turn up a murder weapon in the house.

Some 25 members of the sheriff's reserve were then called in to aid deputies in combing the area for the weapon and clues.

But a search of all the buildings on the farm and fields and roadside ditches near the farm failed to turn up anything. Most of the sheriff's reserve had left the area by mid-afternoon.

A small contingent of regular deputies remained at the scene while others talked with neighbors and followed up leads.

Shortly after 3:00 PM a National Guard helicopter was dispatched from Waterloo to assist in the search and to take film footage of the area to be used in the investigation later.

It was learned that deputies questioned a man late Saturday afternoon who said he picked up a hitchhiker on Union Road near the farm about 1:30 AM

Christensen said every available man in the department would be used in the investigation.

"I can assure you," he emphasized. "We will leave no stone unturned."

The sheriff said investigators would be talking to immediate family members and neighbors to determine the events leading up to the incident and in an attempt to establish a motive.

"There are no suspects at the present time," Christensen said Saturday night.

Also at the murder scene Saturday were Black Hawk County Attorney David Dutton, investigators with the Waterloo police department's criminalistics lab and Cedar Falls detectives.

—Waterloo *Courier*, November 2nd, 1975, Dan Dundon.

George Colthurst, Jorjean's father, spoke about how quickly the investigators found Tom Mark and interviewed him:

"Well, they of course grabbed [Tom] right away too, because the cops thought it was him first. But they soon realized that he could not have put that together like it was, and I guess they had a pretty good alibi for him, or his whereabouts were, so they cleared him…"

(George and Margaret Colthurst interview transcript, July 10, 1980, p. 25.)

10. The Mark Brothers

George Colthurst spoke about Jerry's temper:

"Les talked about when they were growing up, they used to play pool, upstairs, in the old Mark home, there [the homeplace] and they had a room with a pool table upstairs, and Les was short enough that he couldn't make shots. He wasn't tall enough to look over the table, so he dragged a box there, that he shot from. He said 'I still beat Jerry.' And he said, 'he would get so mad, when I beat him, that he would take the pool cue, and ram it into the wall, and punch holes in the plaster. Yep. Les himself noticed that."

(George and Margaret Colthurst interview transcript, July 10, 1980, pp. 11.)

The Colthursts knew the dynamic within the Mark family intimately and spoke at length about it:

Interviewer: How did Les feel about his brothers?

George Colthurst: He never really talked about Jerry. The only thing he ever said about Dick, was that Dick's a nice guy, but Dick's lazy. Well, Dick was always in financial trouble, Wayne was having to subsidize him all along, in fact, Les even loaned Dick some money… (Colthurst transcript, p. 8)

I: How did Les feel about Tom?

GC: During the last few months [before the murders] they [Wayne and Les] had given Les power of attorney with Tom. Because Tom was always driving his car someplace, running out of gas, and leaving it, and the police would impound it, they would take it in, and Les would have to go down and get it straightened out, and try to get his brother straightened out. And finally he just said, "You just can't have it anymore, Tom." You know, you can't have it. And we always thought that Tom was a little flaky. I guess that's about the only word I can think of."

...

I: Why did Les choose Jerry to be his best man? Were they close friends?

Margaret Colthurst: Yes.

GC: Yeah.

I: These teachers [of Les] also told us that Les hero-worshipped Jerry, because Jerry was going to the Peace Corps, was doing this, was doing that. Did you ever have the feeling that he hero-worshipped Jerry as he got older?

MC and GC: No.

MC: He [Les] liked him. But we never felt that he worshipped him, especially the last few years.

I: Why?

MC: Because he [Jerry] wouldn't make anything of himself. He wouldn't discipline himself. Les was a very disciplined person. And when they were in partnership on the farm, Jerry would want to sleep in, goof off—

GC: Go uptown and let dad and Les do the work.

I: Was Jerry all talk and no action?

GC: Well, this school janitor, the day of the funeral, I was in the church, I had come early. And he said, well, all the time they were growing up, I had all these boys on ball teams, good ball teams, he said Les's dad Wayne, Wayne was very concerned about who was gonna take over the reins out there on the farm. Who would take over the business? And he said, "I always told him, Les is your steady one. He is the one you're gonna depend on. He's gonna make it through."

MC: I think that Les lost patience with Jerry, well Les was about nineteen when they were farming, and he lost patience with Jerry because he wouldn't work.

GC: When they got in that argument in May, the letter we got from Jorjean said "Jerry just could not comprehend the fact that this twenty-five year old brother was running eleven hundred acres and making all the decisions."

...

I: Jerry seems to have made a bungle of farming?

GC: Jerry once blew up at the fertilizer supplier, and he [the supplier] just told Wayne and Les, he said, "I'd like to sell you fertilizer, and take care of your needs, but if you're going to have him [Jerry] in your operation, I don't want nothin' to do with it."

...

I: Did Jorjean like Jerry?

GC: She liked his wife [Rebecca] very much. She wished Jerry would settle down and go to work and make something of himself. You know, this was reflected from Les because this guy was bouncing from one thing to another. And of course you know he tried being an attorney for the poor people in Des Moines, and he tried the Peace Corps, and he wanted to go down to Texas and live there, and we know that his dad was feeding him money the whole time, we knew this. Then he goes out to California and separates from his wife, starts livin' with another woman, burned his law books.

I: Burned his law books?

GC: That's what we heard, burned his law books, said he would never wear a necktie again, did the whole hippie bit, and I think you've gotta look at his background.

All the years he was growing up, he was momma's pet. And if he wasn't number one, she changed the rules so he was.

I: She [Dorothy] preferred Jerry to Les?

GC: Yes.

I: Her favorite?

GC: Yes.

I: Why?

GC: She was his pet, Les was his dad's favorite.

(George and Margaret Colthurst interview transcript, July 10, 1980, pp. 9-14)

11. Ride West

During the November 3rd South Lake Tahoe Interview with Detective Newman, Jerry Mark insisted that he had stayed in Chappell, Nebraska on Friday night and left there Saturday morning to drive his motorcycle to Cheyenne, where he picked up a ride from a trucker.

Here is testimony from Jerry Mark and Merrilyn Forrest during that interview:

N: Friday night, about what time did you stay there? [in Chappell, Nebraska]

JM: Oh, I went to bed—you know I killed the whole day Friday—I didn't get anywhere Friday—Wednesday and Thursday I burned up the road Friday I had just been so groggy and stuff—it was a dumb thing because this was a very unplanned trip—one of my goals was to just play it by ear and I wanted to get back in touch with myself and I wanted to—to think things over about our plans and I've been looking for work and I wanted to—to give myself a new—you know I haven't had a lot of luck finding the job I've wanted to have...

N: It's tough—

JM:... and—and uh—and also they were both in the middle of divorces, you know, and there's a lot of—a lot of things involved in that—'course my hearing was just about to come up and—and uh—and if I'd have just stayed down there in the Mojave Desert area, you know, and just kind drank a few beers and relaxed and—and thought things over and been at a place where Mimi could have gotten ahold of me everything would have been okay, you know, she wouldn't have gotten upset and her family and, you know lots of people... but-but-it just uh...

MF: Didn't you try to call me that night, the next morning?

JM. Oh, yeah, when I got up—when I got up and I slept, boy I slept like a log that night—'cause I was so pooped.

N: Uh huh.

JM: And uh I tried to call you [Mimi] that night too, but you weren't... and I couldn't stay up—I know you were out—gonna be out with [inaudible] and you said if I was gonna call you real late I could... but I slept until around 9:00 or 9:30 that morning and when I got up I went... I hadn't cleaned up all this time—I had no time, I was just bumming it and there was an opportunity to get a hot sink wash and hot shave and the attendant was there cleaning up and we sort of exchanged, you know how you talk to somebody—casual situation—

N: This was in Chappell?

JM: That was the place I stayed that night—

N: Okay, there's a gas station you say there?

JM: No, this was that Nebraska rest area—it's a regular…

N: Yeah, but you said something about—didn't you say something about a gas station or, where this guy worked?

JM: No, he was in the rest area…

N: Oh, maintenance man?

JM: Maintenance man, that's it! I meant the attendant, you know, he… all those guys in—in Nebraska wear these—they have orange suits—I saw a couple of 'em in different rest areas you know, they either have an orange or yellow suit—they drive these little orange pickups and uh—you know they go from rest area to rest area and clean urinals and stuff—mop the floors…

N: Did you get his name or… ?

JM: Goodness, no, no—it was just one of those deals, when I walked in he was moppin' in the stool area and I say am I gonna be in your way, and he said naw, go ahead and I shaved… there may have been mention of the—of the Nebraska football game too because uh, Nebraska was playing Missouri—Saturday and uh…

N: What time did you leave there?

JM: Well, I left there uh—I tried to call her first—well no, I don't think there was a phone there—I don't remember whether there was a phone there or not but uh, I probably didn't get out of there until around 10:30 or 11:00 sometime.

N: Where did you head to from there?

JM: Headed back—well, I headed down the road first because I had to go down the road, there wasn't a turnaround there and I don't know whether I took the first turnaround or the second one because I was I think I was lookin' for a gas station to tank up on gas too and stuff but my basic intent was to turn around and go back up through Cheyenne and places 'cause I heard, you know, you listen to these drivers—truck drivers are a tremendous source of information about the roads. .

N: Uh huh.

JM: And there was supposedly—it was supposedly gonna—it wasn't a lot of snow, it was a light snow and—and uh—they said the roads were clearing, you know, so—

N: You headed up towards Cheyenne Wyoming, then?

JM: Back—back towards Cheyenne—uh, I drove well, this was so—this was a frustrating thing—I would go from every rest area to rest area or every exit no matter what the exit was, I'd exit and place a call to Mimi 'cause I was 'cause that very evening we were supposed to go to this party and uh.

N: Now this is November 1st?

JM: This is, this is Saturday—

N: Yeah.

JM: Right.

N: The 1st?

JM: Right—and there I am trying to get back home and uh—but also I gotta let her know about this party—she's and uh, you know, what's happened to me 'cause uh—although I –I really—we weren't –we weren't supposed to get in touch Friday night 'cause you… she [Mimi] was going out with her sister-in-law

N: Uh huh—was there much snow on the ground?

JM: But—uh, no none at all in Nebraska—it didn't snow at all in Nebraska.

N: Uh huh.

JM: There was a—by the time I got back to Cheyenne there was just traces of—of snow on the roadways—there was absolutely—the roads were perfectly clear and dry, and of course there was snow up in the mountains…

N: So you left from Chappell, Nebraska, to go up towards uh, Cheyenne, Wyoming?

JM: Right—basically I was—I was on the—

N: Do you recall…

JM: I was on the eastbound lanes of the road, I mean this—this rest stop is on the eastbound lane and uh—so I had to go on down eastbound and I went—I know I went on down eastbound far enough to either get gas or food or something 'cause I went down east, well I didn't go down very far—I turned around at one of the turnarounds and came back up, you know, and uh—then spent from then until uh, whatever time I called your mother here [in South Lake Tahoe] which she had written down—spent going from—I had—I didn't make very good time the first part of the day on Saturday because uh—1:30 from then until 1:30 I went off every exit and tried to call her to let her know where I was and what was going on and uh—except for one time when uh—uh—I had—things were starting to go wrong the motorcycle—little things, I had slipped on the ice in Wyoming, pulling out of a truck stop and dumped it and I broke a—I have a footrest you know, and I didn't realize I had broke it, but I kept hearing this vibrating noise—it was broke right at the bolt, you know, when I would—certain up-amps on the motorcycle would cause it to vibrate and make this noise and I started—I thought something was wrong with one of the valves or something was going wrong with the motorcycle, started trying to mess up so I killed some time that way too, but uh—anyway uh—well I'd been you know I just basically—I got back—I got back…

N: You were on the highway you were on when you left to go towards Cheyenne?

JM: Cheyenne's on Interstate 80—

N: Oh, it is?

JM: Right, I know it was—I'm just basically retracing my steps now –I went back up to Cheyenne and I went to the Little America truck stop there—'cause it was so cold and I hung around there trying to find somebody—some truck driver who had uh space on his truck to load my motorcycle on and I wanted to pay somebody to haul me over the mountains 'cause it—it had been so miserable coming across them before, you know—and I found a guy—along about, uh, I don't know what time it was, whether it was around 11:00 or 12:00 or midnight, I don't remember—it was—it was toward, you know it was around the midnight area—

N: Uh huh.

JM: For the life of me I don't know what time it was…

N: Were you staying at this little America truck stop in Cheyenne?

JM: I was hanging out there—I was hanging out there—

N: Looking for someone

JM: Looking for

[TAPE ENDS]

(Police interview transcript, November 3, pp. 8-12.)

Jayathan Hurd was an attendant at the Boondocks in Williams, Iowa, some 80 miles from Finchford. He was working the graveyard shift, 11:00 PM to 7:00 AM, and testified that Jerry Mark rode in sometime between 3:30 and 5:00 the morning of November 1st. He was able to pick Mark out of a police lineup in Waterloo.

Dutton: Mr. Hurd, do you remember how much gas you put in that motorcycle at that time?

Hurd: It was close to two gallons.

D: Do you remember what the total sale was in dollars?

H: It was around $1.24.

D: Now, Mr. Hurd, while you were filling it up, where was the man that rode in on that motorcycle.

H: Right beside his cycle.

D: And where was he from where you were standing?

H: That would be about three foot, at the most.

D: What, if anything, happened as you completed filling the motorcycle and putting the gas hose away?

H: I spilled a little gas on his tank.

D: And as you spilled gas on the tank, did the rider say anything to you?

H: Yes. He pulled a grease rag out of my pocket and he said, "You sons of bitches don't know how to do anything right."

D: Okay. And did he proceed to wipe up the gas spilled at that time?

H: Yes, he did.

D: Were you able to understand clearly what he said, both at the time he asked for the gas and also the time he made that comment to you?

H: Yes, sir.

D: How did he speak, as you remember it?

H: It was a soft voice.

(Trial transcript, Book X, pp. 2318-9.)

Directly contradicting Mark's alibi story, Mark Van Housen testified that he waited on Jerry Mark on Saturday morning, November 1st. Housen worked at a DX station in Aurora, Nebraska, some 250 miles east of Chappell. Housen testified, oddly enough, for the defense, saying that he thought Jerry rode in around 10:00 that morning, thereby making it difficult for him to have ridden the nearly 400 miles from Finchford by that time. Here is part of his testimony:

Defense lawyer John Sandre: And did you then go out to service [the motorcyclist, identified as Jerry Mark)

Van Housen: Yes, I did.

JS: And what did you do at that point?

VH: Proceeded out to where he had parked and asked if I could fill it up with gas, and he said he just filled up back a ways, nodded his head toward the west, and said it wouldn't take much gas, but he would squeeze in what he could. He was mostly concerned with his oil had been giving him problems. [sic] … we finally found an old beer bottle back behind the station, and I had to clean that out, and then we dumped some of the oil in there.

JS: And then, as I understand it, you put the oil in there and stuffed a rag in there?

VH: Correct.

JS: Did you see what this individual did with the oil?

VH: He had a square tote bag back behind him on the seat and he put it in there.

(Trial Transcript, Book XII, pp. 2730, ff.)

However, Dutton pointed out that Van Housen was asked to remember the time of Mark's visit some two months after it happened, so he may easily have misremembered the exact time. Dutton's assertion was given credence by the fact that Mark called Mimi's mother from Alda, Nebraska, just 35 miles away from Aurora, around 1:30 that afternoon. This time and location was documented by phone company records.

Larry Rauch, the trucker who gave Jerry Mark a ride starting in Cheyenne, Wyoming, offered the following testimony during the trial.

Dutton: Where did he [the Defendant] make contact with you, Mr. Rauch?

Rauch:... I put gas in the truck and I was in paying for it, and we was in kind of a station house, separate to the truck stop area. And that's when he come up and asked me.

D: What did he ask you?

R: He asked me where I was going to. I told him I was going to Seattle.

D: Did he at that time request transportation?

R: He said that he was going that way and if I would give him a ride.

D: What was your initial response?

R: Ah, at first I didn't want to take him, because I had planned on taking the trip by myself, and my pickup was kind of full in the front.

D: All right. He continued to talk to you, and what caused you to change your mind, if you did?

R: I had never been out West before, and I didn't know the best way to get to Seattle, and he said that he could show me an excellent way to get there, and it wouldn't be out of my way at all.

D: Did he have any maps or did he profess any experience with that particular path or route?

R: No, he didn't have no maps... He said he knew the way.

D: All right. Did you agree to give him a ride?

R: Yes.

D: And about what time of the evening then did you leave Cheyenne, Wyoming, with the Defendant?

R: Oh, it was roughly 10:30 that evening.

D: Mr. Rauch, what, if any, transportation did the Defendant have at the Little America Truck Stop in Cheyenne?

R: He had a motorcycle.

D: What was done with the motorcycle?

R: The motorcycle was brought and put in the horse trailer.

D: And was it tied down, or was that necessary in any way?

R: Yes, it was tied down.

D: Mr. Rauch, what was the appearance of the Defendant when you saw him at that truck stop and as you later saw him in your pickup on that evening?… what about his appearance did you notice or remember when you first saw him?

R: He looked a little chilly and cold.

D: Had he recently shaved, or could you tell?

R: No, not really. He had one or two days' growth on him.

D: Did you ask him any questions as to how he happened to be out there on a motorcycle in November of 1975?

R: Yes, sir. I thought it was kind of strange, so I asked him, and he said that him and his wife was getting a divorce and he just got a wild hair up his ass and decided to take off and do a little thinking about it.

D: All right. Did he tell you how far he had gone, where he had been before he came back to the Cheyenne truck stop?

R: He said he went up into the Nebraska panhandle.

D: And did he ever indicate what his intent was as to which route he was going to take?

R: There was some mention about he was taking another route back, but he stopped at a truck stop and somebody told him that route was snowed in, and he decided to come back this way.

D: Did he indicate whether or not that was the same route he had taken out?

R: No, sir.

D: Did he ever tell you whether or not he had ever gone any further east than the Panhandle of Nebraska?

R: No.

D: How long did this trip take where he accompanied you from Cheyenne, Wyoming?

R: It took about 9, 9-1/2 hours.

D: And will you indicate to the Jury what the Defendant was doing?

R: Well, as it was chilly out, I had the heater on in the pickup and he dozed off a couple of times. We had a little conversation.

D: Did he sleep during the trip for periods of hours?

R: No, not for periods of hours. Just dozed here and there.

D: Where was it that you and he parted company then after this 9-1/2 hours?

R: It was a junction outside of Ogden, Utah. I believe it's where I wanted to go north to Seattle.

D: And did he direct you in any way as to which road or which fork to take?

R: Yes.

D: And what did he say, if you remember?

R: Well, he took me right to the spot. He told me I wanted to go north, and that he would go this way.

D: Did he pay you anything for the trip from Cheyenne to Ogden?

R: He gave me, I believe, $45.00. I took five dollars and give it back to him and said, "You take this; you might need it."

D: Okay, and did he ever mention during the nine-hour trip that he had grown up and lived near Cedar Falls, Iowa?

R: No.

D: Did he ever mention Waterloo, Iowa?

R: No.

D: Did he ever mention his father or any farming operation in that vicinity?

R: No.

D: Did you on the date of November 1, 1975, ever hear of anything about four members of the Leslie Mark family being murdered earlier that morning.

R: No, sir.

...

D: Did he seem cool and relaxed, calm?

R: Yes.

(Trial Transcript, Vol. X, pp. 2394, ff.)

14. Leslie Mark Family Funeral

The Waterloo *Courier* printed this story on the day of the funeral:

Cedar Falls—Four members of a rural Cedar Falls family—slain Saturday in one of Iowa's most brutal mass murders—were buried Tuesday afternoon in a tiny pioneer cemetery overlooking their home.

The burial of the four members of the Leslie Mark family came as officers from four law enforcement agencies struggled to unearth cues into the execution-style slaying.

Mr. and Mrs. Mark, both age 25, and their two children, Julie, 5, and Jeffrey, 21 months, were buried in a small country cemetery less than a mile from where they were slain.

The burial followed services at a Cedar Falls church which were attended by almost 1,000 persons. Several hundred persons attended the burial in the Gerholdt Cemetery northwest of the city.

A number of plainclothes police officers were among the mourners at both the church and at the cemetery.

The funeral for the Mark family was held in the Cedar Falls Trinity United Methodist Church.

A crowd of several hundred people lined the street in front of the colonial style church 30 minutes before the services began.

The congregation jammed a main floor and balcony area, as well as the full basement of the building.

One of Leslie Mark's brothers, Richard Mark, a minister in Winnipeg, Canada, assisted the Rev. Harold J. Burris, pastor of the church, in officiating during both the funeral and graveside services.

Rev. Mark delivered the eulogy in memory of his brother's family, describing them as "good, honest, hard workers who liked the neighborhood in which they lived and would help out any man who asked."

"They loved the earth. They were special people who only come along once in a lifetime," the Rev. Mr. Mark said.

He said the family had been sustained throughout the tragedy by telegrams, letters, and phone calls from "all parts of the continent."

In the only reference during the services to the murders, Rev. Mark asked the congregation "to pray for the person responsible for this tragedy, God be merciful to them or him."

More than 100 bouquets banked the sides of the church behind and beside the four unopened caskets, which lined the front of the sanctuary.

A neighbor who had come to the Mark farm to pick corn early Saturday morning discovered the bodies of Leslie Mark, his wife and two children.

The murders are under the investigation of the Cedar Falls and Waterloo police departments, the Black Hawk County sheriff's office and the Bureau of Criminal Investigation.

No positive leads had been uncovered late Tuesday, BCI agents who were co-coordinating the investigation said.

(Waterloo *Courier*, Wednesday, November 5, 1975.)

Dick Mark, the oldest brother and an ordained minister, offered this eulogy at the funeral:

We have gathered together at the church, the Christian community, to celebrate the life and death of the Leslie Mark family, to celebrate the significance and meaning of their family, and to offer their lives to the family of God and to all creation. Death is a very living part of man's life and no life is finished without the experience of death. Death is the crucial point in the human adventure, which somehow transposes every other aspect of life. Death is to be received in humble gratitude and must ever be honored in honest dignity.

I like to say something like this: Sainthood begins at death. The gifts and great qualities and joyous moments and significant occasions that you and I share together, these are the things that sustain us at moments and particularly low points that are on our journey in life and as we journey through life.

We had the opportunity as the Colthursts and the Marks and some of our family and friends to sit down and rehearse and share with one another the kind of gifts and qualities that Les and Jorjean and Julie and Jeff had. I just have a random selection, and you probably have many more experiences.

They were good honest hard workers, had lots of friends. They enjoyed working. They were responsible. They liked their neighborhood. They would help any man out. They were a close family, a loving family. They enjoyed kids and especially they enjoyed their own. They were good church workers. Somebody said that Les was probably a born farmer. He loved the earth. They were special people—perhaps those that only come along once in a few generations. They took things seriously and yet had a bit of laughter about them. They were full of life. Matter of fact, it was kind of a bubbly laughter that Les and that Jorjean would have (and sometimes Les, you will remember, would laugh with a slap on the knee). They were aggressive, enthusiastic, "real goers". They planned for the future. Their children—Julie (whom I always called a princess) she'd go anywhere with her dad or mom. Jeff was always into things—always ate, always had to eat the bad food first before he would have a dish of ice cream. The parents were patient, good teachers, worked well. Jorjean was one who had exquisite taste. And it has been told that she robbed the food money to buy a little knickknack, a décor item, or flowers.

Well, we have many, many moments, many events that come to mind, and it's these kinds of moments and occasions that sustain us at a moment like this. These are qualities of sainthood. But I suspect that if I would mention or rather if I were to call my brother and sister-in-law saints, they would probably sit up and laugh at me.

God has been good and He has blessed us even in the midst of tragedy. He'd given us a family of four, Les, Jorjean, Julie and Jeff, who have enriched and blessed our lives. They've given us significant moments and great occasions to be with them. They've given assistance, help, and support. They've allowed and endeavored us to live a rich life. We've been blessed because we've been a part of their community, and they've been blessed because we've been a part of theirs.

God has been good to us, too, in this time because we've been enriched and blessed by the care and support of family, friends, neighbors, relatives, churches, literally all across the continent. We've been blessed by telegrams, telephone calls, flowers, food, condolences which have come from all parts, literally all parts of this continent. And for that we're greatly thankful. Your prayers have undergirded us. God's presence is here. Your assistance and care was gratefully received, and it is deeply needed at this time.

I never wrote many letters to Les, he and I would get on the telephone and both of our wives would get upset at the telephone bills we had. But there was always one thing (as in one of the last letters he wrote to my brother, and in all his conversations with me) one of his great concerns was always care for the future—whether that was family, his family, friends, or what he was going to do. It was always a care for the future, so I have some recommendations which are for the care of the future. One is that you spend this day with us; the burial will be at Gerholdt Cemetery near the Mark farm, and there will be a reception following at the church basement here. Plan to stay with us and visit with us and enjoy yourself, and celebrate this day. Secondly, we ask that you pray for the Les Mark family. They have lived and celebrated their life and death and now begin a great new journey, a new future. Thirdly, we would ask that you pray for those or that person that's responsible for this tragedy. God's mercy be with them or him. Fourthly, we would ask that you pray for the Colthurst and Mark families and relatives and friends; for it is the spirit power that comes from prayer that undergirds and sustains our living. Fifthly, come and visit and stop in. I have to say something like this—we ask not for your sorrow or for your remorse—we ask for you care, concern, and help for the future; a friendly smile, a pleasant word, a treat to eat, or a hand of assistance. And sixthly, we ask that you pick up and use some of the qualities of the Les Mark family. Probably you can name more than I do but I just wrote down three: pick up their bubbly spirit, their future oriented vision, their relaxed but joyful style.

So this day we offer this family unto the family of God and to all creation. We place them gladly and gratefully on behalf of all good men everywhere in the hands of God, in the hands of whom they were already, that mysterious power who rules the unknown realm of death. The Lord of history will care for them.

God moves in a mysterious way, his wonders to perform;

He plants his footsteps on the sea and rides upon the storm;
Blind unbelief is sure to err, and scan his work in vain;
God is his own interpreter and he shall make it plain.

This we offer in the name of the Father, and of the Son, and of the Holy Ghost.

Amen.

(Eulogy spoken and given to the families, November 4, 1975.)

16. Questioning Mimi

Dorothy spoke about Mimi's arrest:

Jerry came [home] without Mimi. [After they were questioned on Friday] And that was the most idiotic thing and he knows it now. They said, "Well we've got a little more to ask her." And so I went right to the phone and called up and I got Jaeger [Loras Jaeger, Cedar Falls Police Detective] and I said, "Why is she being kept?"

"Well,… she's just taken a lie detector test." So I said, "All right, I'll be right down and get her."

"Oh, no, Mrs. Mark, it's our business to take her home and we'll have her home by 3:00." Come 3:00 and she wasn't home. I call up again. "Well, we'll have her home by 5:00 and maybe she's taking a lie detector test." They fed me one lie after the other. Uh, she told me that the first time I called, she'd already taken the lie detector test.

Well, finally, "We're going to keep her all night." I don't know with Jerry being a lawyer why he didn't get himself right back down there. Why I didn't say to him, "Get down there!" Why Sindlinger didn't go for us. We were too naïve!

They kept her five days. They didn't charge her. They kept her part of the time in the city jail, part of the time in the county jail. They interrogated her all the time and she has a very fragile personality. And she goes to pieces. And they fed her stuff. For instance, they said to her, "Did you know that the reason Jerry came back in May was to come back to farm?" And her answer was, "Was he going to do that?" Her answer wasn't like I think I would have answered is "No he didn't—you're wrong." But hers was, "Is that why he came back?" Never saying, "No, he came back because his father called him saying he was dying." Well, his father was dying, but not for a year and a half after. Uh, they didn't give her a toothbrush."

(Dorothy Mark interview transcripts, July 14, 1980, p. 20.)

188

18. Failed Polygraph

On Wednesday, November 12, 1975, Gary Marker, the polygraph examiner submitted the following report on Merrilyn Forrest. He conducted the polygraph examination on November 7, Friday, and Merrilyn was arrested after that test.

Procedure:

The subject willingly submitted to an examination and the usual procedures were employed in conducting this type of examination. The examination was conducted in the Bureau office in Waterloo, Iowa, on the afternoon of November 7, 1975.

Results:

During pretest interview, subject advised that she had known Jerry approximately one year. She advised that she had known about Jerry wanting to take a motorcycle trip to clear his head for some time. She advised that on Sunday, October 26th, she told Jerry "why don't you go on your trip and I'll give you some money." She advised that before the trip he had spent some of the money to buy a motorcycle suit and some other things that he needed. She advised that she thought he had approximately $70 when he left on this trip, however, he had taken all of his food with him. She advised that when he returned he had a can of spam left. She advised that before the trip they had discussed approximately where he was going to ride and he was supposed to go to Southern California and the desert and he was going to come back up to the California-Nevada and talked about meeting at Merrilyn's parents' house. He was supposed to be back sometime Saturday, November 1, 1975. She advised that on October 29th the landlord had advised her that a shed belonging to them had been broken into. She advised that she did not go down to check to see if anything was missing at that time. She advised that Jerry called her on October 29th and 30th. During one of those conversations she advised him of the break-in and he asked her to go down and see what was missing. On Saturday, November 1st, after she had found out about the tragedy in Iowa her brother did go to the shed and discovered that a revolver and an Iowa license plate were missing. Both these items belonged to Jerry and Merrilyn. She advised that at this time that she felt that Jerry might have come to Iowa and killed the Leslie Mark family. She advised that during conversation with Becky, Jerry's ex-wife, she had related some concern for her and her two children, and that Jerry might be capable of doing something like this referring to the Leslie Mark family. She advised that Jerry does not like to spend money for anything, and that he hates to throw anything away that he might have to replace. After Jerry returned she discussed the trip with him advising him that she was worried about him and that he would have to substantiate where he had been because of the tragedy in Iowa. He [sic] advised that they have not talked about his trip since then.

She advised that on the 29th Jerry had advised her that he left approximately 10:00 AM She stated that she had left approximately 8:00 that morning and was not sure what time he left. She advised that he had made some reference as to going down to the shed and getting some things in preparation for his trip, however, she did now know what items these would be. Throughout the interview she kept referring to the circumstantial evidence which made her believe that Jerry might be involved in this tragedy, and to the mistakes that Jerry made while he was on this trip. She advised that after talking with Jerry on Sunday, November 2nd, she did not suspect him of committing these homicides.

Subject was given three specific tests concerning this investigation. Following are the relevant questions utilized during these tests and her answers.

Do you suspect Jerry of shooting the Mark family? No
Do you know for sure if Jerry shot any of the Mark family? No
Before Jerry left, did you know he was going to Iowa? No
When Jerry returned from his trip, did he tell you he had been in Iowa? No
When Jerry left did you know for sure if he had a gun? No
Did Jerry tell you when he threw his sweatshirt away? No

There were specific reactions to relevant questions utilized during these tests.

Subject appeared to show a more specific reaction to "do you know for sure if Jerry shot any of the Mark family?" rather than "Do you suspect Jerry of shooting the Mark family?"

Conclusion:

After careful examination of this subjects polygrams, it is the opinion of this examiner the subject was not telling the complete truth at the time of the examination.

(Signed) Gary Marker, Special Agent

19. Arrest

Dorothy described her feelings and reactions as Jerry was arrested:

I was dumbfounded when he was arrested. I thought somebody would tell me. And Mr. Sindlinger came out, he was out here just about the same time. I was in the kitchen, Wayne was in his office the windows look right out on the yard. Jerry was out cleaning up my peonies and cleaning up the yard when they came, Mr. Sindlinger came too. I do not know, I think he drove in right after the sheriff, whether someone in the sheriff's office called him, whether Dutton called him, I don't know. Uh, but he came out to tell us and I went as soon as he told me I went out the door but they were gone with Jerry. Maybe it's a good thing I didn't see them.

(Dorothy Mark interview transcript, p. 20)

23. Trial I

During the trial, David Dutton questioned Alga Forrest, Merrilyn's former husband, concerning the Mark family. Mr. Forrest described conversations that took place between he and Jerry Mark about Jerry's father, about their relationship and how it evolved.

Dutton: Mr. Forrest, during the time that you lived next door to the Defendant, did you ever have occasion to visit with him about his background, about where he had come from, about his family, about his personal life and his plans?

Forrest: Yes.

D: And did he tell you about this father's business and his father's wealth or general condition?

F: Yes.

D: What did he tell you?

F: He said he had several hundred or thousand acres and worth several million. I remember he said his father was dying of cancer, I believe.

D: Did he ever indicate whether or not he had ever worked on the farm or been part of the farming operation?

F: Yes, I guess he had worked on the farm for years, and then when he was in school, he used to come back on the weekends and on his time off and worked on the farm.

D: Had he ever owned or expected to own any portion of that farmland, did he indicate?

F: He said he had expected to.

D: How much had he expected to acquire as a result of his efforts or labors on the farm?

F: He said he expected about half of it.

D: Did he say what had happened to his expectation of owning half of the farm or obtaining an interest in the farming operation?

F: He said that Les... had screwed him out of his portion of the farm, and that he would never forgive him for it.

D: How did that come up? How did it come up in the conversation that he talked about his younger brother Les about being screwed out of his share of the farm?

F: We were just outside talking about our families, I guess, and different things.

D: And as he spoke... what did you observe about his appearance, about his demeanor and attitude, and the words that he spoke?

F: Oh, he was very depressed about it, I'd say. Unhappy.

D: On how many occasions did he mention the farm and his younger brother and what had happened with regard to losing an interest in the farm?

F: Oh, several times, but there was only a couple that I can pinpoint.

D: Did he ever indicate to you whether Les would acquire the entire farm or part of it or none of it?

F: Oh, he thought Les would acquire the entire farm.

...

D: And during this time, did the Defendant ever talk about his father?

F: Yes.

D: And did he describe his father's activities and how he acquired his wealth?

F: I believe so, somewhat. The main thing was that he [his father] would do anything to get what he wanted; it didn't matter, you know, whose toes he stepped on.

D: Did he say or express how he felt about his father?

F: Yes.

D: Tell us what he said, as best as you remember the Defendant's words.

F: The only think that I can remember him saying about him [Jerry's father] was that he would piss on his grave when he died.

D: And did the Defendant say whether or not he had ever expressed that sentiment to his father, or was he just expressing it to you?

F: He said he had told him.

D: He told his father that?

F: Yes.

(Trial transcript, Book V, pp. 1152-1156)

24. Trial II

Had Jerry Mark taken the stand in his own defense, David Dutton was prepared. Here are his notes for the cross examination that never happened; Dutton worked from his own handwritten outline on a legal pad.

Background as attorney—
high grades

192

courses in criminal law and procedure

worked for legal aid

represented members of American Ind. and [illegible] on criminal matters also studied constitutional law

—Knew that when police were conducting a criminal investig. they started the interview with a warning—

—that you have the right to remain silent

—that anything you say can and will be used against you in a court of law

—that you have a right to be represented by an attorney

—that if you can't afford an attorney one can and will be provided at state expense

—that you can stop answering questions at any time

—You were interviewed by agents of the BCI as part of their investigation of your brother's death

—You were advised of the same rights I have just read

—As an attny. you know of the consequence of making a statement

—You knew the implications of lying to the police

—You agreed to make a statement

—You lied to the police

—You lied in regard to the basic fact in the investigation:

—You lied about where you were at the time of the murders. You were not in Coalinga, Barstow (a little bird didn't...), Las Vegas, Provo, Cheyenne on Fri. (Thurs) Chappell on Fri PM (Thursday PM)

—you lied about how far east you went—

—you lied about where you called MF from—

—you lied about planning a trip to the desert—

—you lied about where you spent Friday night and Saturday AM

—you att, to persuade police that you were too far away to be the murderer—you failed and you lied—

II. With full appreciation of what you were doing you also told the police a series of lies about the motorcycle—

a. That you had only put 2000 to 2,500 miles on it—in fact you disconnected the cable

b. That you had never removed the California license plate

—fingerprints

—bolts

—c. That you didn't take the Iowa plate with you on the trip and use it when you went into Iowa

III. You told the police that the license plate had been stolen from the locker while you were gone—

—how did that aluminum [from the Iowa plate] get on the bracket—

—how did that second bolt mark get on the bracket—

—how did that outline of the Iowa plate get on the bracket-

IV. You said that at the same time these unknown and unreported thieves took the license plate that they took the gun—the same gun used to kill Les and Jorjean, Julie and Jeff.

If both were taken off at the same time and from the same locker will you explain how the license ended up with you on the trip? You had the license plate you must also have had the gun—!

You also lied about the bullets, didn't you—

What did you want to hide by saying you didn't buy the shells

Oct. 20, 1975—where did you go—

What time did you arrive

Use highway 101

Go thru Paso Robles

About noon

Are you saying that someone else using your ID was in PRobles w/i a couple blocks of the road buying the same ammo that killed your brother while you were riding by?

It's also a coincidence that that person bought the odd ammo that was called for on the barrel of the gun you had—

Coincidence that this purchase was w/in 10 days of your brother's death

Coincidence that the gun was taken on the day you left

Coincidence that you got lost on the same weekend that your brother got killed—

Coincidence that the killer knew where the phone lines were to the house—

Coincidence that the same shells purchased 10 days earlier in So.Cal. were found in front of that phone box—

Coincidence that these shells matched shells used to kill your brother and the two boxes at the sport shop from where the shells were purchased—in your name—

Coincidence that you were id. at Brady, Atlantic, Newton, Ackley, Williams, Stuart, Iowa, which just happens to be the most direct route to the homeplace—

25. Verdict

The following article appeared in the Waterloo *Courier* on June 22, 1976:

<u>Faces Life Term for Murders</u>

"Mark convicted in Slayings "

Sioux City—Jerry Allen Mark faces a life sentence in prison as a result of his conviction in district court here Tuesday on four counts of first-degree murder.

Judge Carroll Engelkes set sentencing for July 8 in Black Hawk County.

The case had been moved to Woodbury County on a change of venue.

The verdict was reached about an hour and one half after the jury resumed deliberation Tuesday morning.

The jury began deliberation about 6:30 Monday night and retired about four hours later without reaching a decision.

The jury had four possible verdicts—guilty of first-degree murder, guilty of second degree murder, guilty of manslaughter, or innocent.

First-degree murder in Iowa carries a mandatory life sentence.

Its decision means the state proved beyond a reasonable doubt Mark slew his brother, Leslie, his brother's wife Jorjean, and the couple's two young children Nov. 1.

The bodies of the Leslie Mark family were found riddled with .38 caliber bullets in bedrooms at their rural Cedar Falls home.

Mark, who had been living in Berkeley, Calif., was arrested a few days following the murders after he attended funeral services for his younger brother's family.

Mark showed no visible signs of emotion as the judge read the verdict. After the verdict, Mark was handcuffed and taken into custody by agents of the Iowa Bureau of Criminal Investigation.

As he was led out of the courtroom he embraced his mother, Mrs. Dorothy Mark, and his wife, Merrilyn.

The verdict brings to a close one of the longest, most complex criminal trials in Iowa history.

The jury deliberations were preceded by testimony from 80 prosecution and defense witnesses, some of whom took the stand on more than one occasion.

Including rebuttal testimony, the state called 67 witnesses, of which 27 were from out of state. Prosecution testimony began May 28 with the state resting its case last Wednesday.

The prosecution maintained Mark was driven by greed and jealousy to devise a complex murder plot which involved a three-day motorcycle trip from Berkeley, Calif, to the Cedar Falls farm home of his brother's family.

The defense called 13 witnesses to testify during a two-day period. Mark did not testify in his own defense.

Prior to the start of deliberations, the judge instructed the jurors not to make inferences from the fact Mark did not take the witness stand.

The defense offered no alternative theory for the murders, based on the sighting of a blue car near the Mark farm home during the early morning hours of Nov. 1.

The defense emphasized the failure of the state to find fingerprints, hair, or blood samples at the murder scene which could be traced to Mark.

The circumstantial evidence, the defense contended, was not sufficient to convict Mark. The lengthy prosecution case was based primarily on the investigation at the Mark home, analysis of bullets found at the murder scene and eyewitnesses to the defendant's 2000-mile motorcycle journey.

The state also brought in a witness from California who testified a man who gave the name and showed an Iowa driver's license of Jerry Mark bought a box of .38 caliber bullets from him a few days before the slayings.

(Waterloo *Courier*, Dan Dundon, Tuesday, June 22, 1976)

26. Appeals

Here is Jerry Mark's statement on Feb. 20, 1980 after losing his appeal to the Iowa Supreme Court:

I reject the Iowa Supreme Court decision which denied my appeal. As an innocent man, I have no moral nor legal duty to submit to wrongful imprisonment.

I was well raised by my family to believe in justice, to obey the law, and to respect courts and judges. I was taught in school that the foundation of our nation was firmly set upon the fair and equal application of the rule of law.

As a Peace Corps volunteer overseas, I took pride in explaining our Bill of Rights which guarantees the rights of individuals against incursions by the state, powerful interests or impassioned tides of public reaction.

When I became an attorney, I swore upon my oath, just as judges do, to protect the rule of law and to defend the constitutional and legal rights of individuals. Even when as a poverty lawyer, I became disillusioned by the bias in the legal system, favoring the rich and powerful over working people, the less powerful, and the poor, I did not lose my faith in the basic integrity of the courts.

When I was arrested and charged with murder, I was confident the mistake would be corrected. After all, I had been taught that our legal system would not imprison an innocent man. When I was released on pretrial bond, and allowed to live a reasonably normal life for half a year, I felt it was the first step toward clearing me of charges.

As each element of the contrived circumstantial evidence was examined and discredited, my confidence grew that there was no danger of a false conviction.

While out on bond, waiting to be cleared of charges, my over-riding reaction was embarrassment, not fear of imprisonment. I found how extremely embarrassing it is to lose the precious privacy we all take for granted, and to be subject[ed] to horrible accusations and publicity.

My embarrassment was greatest at the trial. My response was to withdraw, to become passive. I wished fruitlessly to awaken from the nightmare of accusation and negative publicity. My reaction was so severe that it was necessary to take tranquilizers for the trial, for the only time in my life.

I did not realize it was necessary to prove my innocence. I was naïve about the effect of prejudice against any man accused in a highly publicized case.

Even when contrived evidence, proven unreliable in pretrial hearings, was allowed by the judge, I remained certain I would be cleared of the charges. My certainty was based on a central principle of justice, that a man is presumed to be innocent unless proven to be guilty beyond any reasonable doubt. Because physical evidence at the murder scene implicated the driver of a blue automobile who apparently left his fingerprints and hair strands in the master bedroom, I was confident the jury would not wrongly convict me.

Thus, it was a terrible shock when I was convicted falsely. Even worse, was the shock of imprisonment. Without the love and support of my family and friends, these shocks would have destroyed me.

As soon as I had adjusted to the prison situation, I wanted to speak out to the public and the legal community about the injustices which had caused my imprisonment.

However, attorneys convinced me to stay silent, because it was felt that the passage of time would settle the passions and cure the publicity and prejudice. I became persuaded that all the Iowa Supreme Court needed was a better environment of public opinion, in order to correct the injustices, reverse the illegal conviction and restore me to my rightful freedom.

I also became confident that my attorney's appeal would be considered fairly. After all, the appeal did not turn on technical violations of abstract constitutional rights, but rather it challenged the basic credibility of all the contrived circumstantial evidence which had been used illegally against me. Applying simple common sense would be adequate to reverse the conviction and to give me justice.

Now, for reasons known only to them, the Iowa Supreme Court has refused to consider my appeal. Justice has again been denied to me. My appeal was not considered fairly. I remain imprisoned for a crime committed by someone else. Thus, it is time for me to speak out.

My life is being taken from me, illegally, day by day. An innocent man has no legal nor moral duty to comply with illegal deprivation of liberty. If my imprisonment becomes permanent, if I have been denied justice after all my legal remedies have been exhausted, I shall no longer submit to this unlawful detention.

Nor shall I attempt to escape like a criminal.

Rather than comply with unlawful imprisonment or attempt any criminal escape, I shall exercise non-violent disobedience to my imprisonment. In essence, the state of Iowa will have to kill me in order to carry out this unlawful detention.

My first course of action, if my imprisonment ever becomes permanent, will be not to eat until I die.

If I am not allowed to die in that manner, I will attempt open escape, in broad daylight, over the wall surrounding this penitentiary. I expect the officers on duty to shoot me, in that event. However, if I am allowed over the wall, I will walk away, not run.

I will not put any person in jeopardy of injury, except myself. I will not use stealth, violence or force, nor will I allow any person to assist me.

I will simply use my life to exercise disobedience against an imprisonment which is both legally and morally wrong.

Illegal detention of an innocent man degrades the human values of all people. All ought to abhor the injustice I am suffering.

[signed] Jerry Mark

At that time, he added this Addendum:

I, Jerry Allen Mark, upon my oath and subject to the full penalties of perjury, do hereby affirm, state and swear that all the statements of fact in the Petition for Rehearing I have prepared pro se are true to the best of my knowledge and belief, and obviously the facts I have stated of my personal knowledge and activity are without qualification attached.

I further affirm, state, and swear that the following facts are truly stated, under the same penalty of perjury:

I did not kill my brother Les, sister-in-law Jorjean, or their children Julie and Jeffey [sic]. I feel I was used as a scapegoat to quiet public alarm and get the frustrated police investigators from under pressure to solve the case.

My family supports me, believes me to be innocent, and knows that because of the quality of relationships that existed in our family that the alleged motives which the prosecution attempted to create are not true.

The only person who accused me of having any ill will toward Les and his family was Alga Forrest, the former husband of my wife, who wrongly believed I had caused a break-up of his marriage. Mr. Forrest was motivated by his hatred of me to lie, and his testimony about my relationship to Les and other family members was false and distorted.

When my family members were murdered, I was on a motorcycle camping trip. Each evening I phoned home to Berkeley, to check in with my wife and assure her I was well, not injured or ill. When she inquired about my whereabouts during these calls, I lied to her about where I was calling from, to avoid her suspicions about whether I had been with another woman, because I had substantially changed direction from my planned trip.

When I was first interviewed by a California police officer about where I had been on my camping trip, my wife and her parents were present. For that reason, and only because of that reason, I foolishly attempted to construct a false itinerary for my camping trip which coincided with the evening reports I had falsely given my wife about my whereabouts.

I was arrested 10 days after the murders. It was during a period of shock and mourning for me and my family. I did not take seriously any possibility that I would be charged with the murders, prior to my arrest, and consequently did not take advantage of that period to locate witnesses who could document my whereabouts on my camping trip; besides, I was asked by police to remain in the Cedar Falls, Iowa area, to cooperate in the investigation, which I agreed to.

It was only after my arrest, and after considerable further delay, that I was given permission to travel out West in the company of my attorney and a private investigator, to attempt to reconstruct my trip while camping and motorcycling. I had no personal means to document my trip, since I had not requested receipts for purchases along the way, had no credit cards (due to closing credit accounts after a recent divorce), and had not visited anyone who knew me while traveling.

We did locate one person who remembered me, due to the most unusual circumstances of our unusual and prolonged contact, and that person was brought as a defense witness to testify on my behalf. I located him from the appearance of the unique gas station at which he worked, and has fortunately remembered a dead raccoon laying sort of behind the station which was still there; and his employer assisted us in locating him. (Witness Van Housen)

The only other prolonged contact I was willing to reveal at that time was with an employee of a horse stable who had given me a ride for approximately six hours in the mountains, carrying my motorcycle in a horse trailer. (Witness Larry Rauch) I had already informed police investigators about him.

I am ashamed that I lied about my itinerary on the camping trip, and even more ashamed for the reasons I was motivated to lie. But, those lies had no relationship to the murder investigation, in motive. I told my wife those lies on the phone before I ever heard about the murders.

However, I hasten to emphasize that I have never lied about my whereabouts or any other fact while under oath.

ODOMETER

I disconnected the odometer on my Honda 450 motorcycle on occasions when traveling, besides when tearing the machine down for servicing it and for fun. The first trip on which I disconnected the odometer was when I rode the cycle down to central California, a distance of several hundred miles, to visit my daughters and to give them rides on my new "toy." The second time was during a portion of my camping trip, until I became concerned about whether the moisture and dew overnight the first evening would cause rust or deterioration of the odometer cable and speedometer mechanisms which were exposed by the disconnection.

My only purpose in disconnecting the odometer cable was to keep the odometer reading low for resale value.

One effect of unhooking the odometer cable is to stop the speedometer from indicating speed of travel. It is illogical for anyone to contend that I disconnected the odometer cable to cover up a secret trip to Iowa for criminal activity. If a person was attempting to make a secret trip, he would be most concerned about avoiding a speeding ticket, and the risk of getting a speeding ticket would be very great without a speedometer for a guide.

LICENSE PLATE

At no time did I put an Iowa license plate on my 450 Honda motorcycle, which was licensed in California. I did take apart the license plate assembly, along with about every other part of the machine after I purchased it used, for servicing, cleaning, getting familiar with it, etc. I specifically recall debating whether to discard or keep the aluminum dealer identification plate which fit on with the license plate, and decide [sic] to put it back on. Testimony at my trial about the license plate assembly undoubtedly relates to how I tore the bike down while servicing and cleaning it, and not to support any false claim that I switched the plate.

CUTTING PHONE WIRES

Tests conducted by the State Crime Lab proved that the pliers I took on my camping trip were not used to cut the phone wires at Les' place. Apparently, this was about the only expert test that they were afraid to distort, since it could be repeated and subjected to disproof. Because of that test, the statement in the Opinion that I cut the phone wires is false, and no reasonable jury could find. [sic]

OTHER EVIDENCE IGNORED

The version of evidence asserted by the prosecution and adopted by the Court ignores physical evidence at the crime scene and corroborated eyewitness testimony at the crime scene which is inconsistent with falsely convicting me.

There was human hair not belonging to Les, Jorjean, Julie, Jeffey, [sic] or me found in the bed clothing of Jorjean's bed, as well as on a rug at bedside.

There were numerous fingerprints not belonging to Les, Jorjean, Jeffey, [sic] or me and also not belonging to any investigator or family member or friend who had business being in that house, and the area in which these fingerprints were found in greatest concentration was in the bedroom of Les and Jorjean, where they were murdered.

There was physical evidence in the bedroom and on Jorjean's body that she had been subject to sodomy shortly before her death. [Neither prosecution nor defense pursued this fact as part of their investigations.]

There were repeated sightings of a dark blue automobile by numerous persons whose descriptions of the auto are consistent with one another, and when that auto was apparently casing the farmstead, cruising past the farmstead erratically, speeding out the driveway [sic] and away from the farmstead in the early morning hours, and subsequently lurking at a distance observing the general scene.

All these forms of evidence are in the record of my trial.

Because the prosecution forced me to physically submit to having hair torn from my head, underarms, chest, and pubic area, in a fruitless attempt to connect the hair found in Jorjean's bed clothing to me, I know that evidence had been regarded as important.

Because I was forced to submit to a fingerprinting session for a period of over several hours, on every surface of my hands repeatedly, I am certain the unidentified fingerprints in the master bedroom were regarded by investigators as important.

In the interests of Justice, I beg the Court to carefully reconsider my appeal. In light of concrete physical evidence at the scene of the crime, inconsistent with the circumstantial evidence which was conjured up to convict me falsely, a reversal is required. In re Winship, 397 US 398, Jackson v. Virginia, 39 CCH S. CT. Bull. 3909 (June 28, 1978).

[Signed] Jerry Allen Mark

Vi-Vim case in 1976-78:

Several stories in the Waterloo *Courier* in 1976 and 1977 detailed the unethical behavior of Leo Baker and Bill Sindlinger, who, with Wayne Mark, conspired to swindle local citizens out of their property at considerable profit to themselves.

The Waterloo *Courier* published the complete text of Judge Richardson's decision in the Leo Baker case on Sunday, July 30, 1978. The judge describes in detail how the "Vi-Vim" corporation (Wayne Mark's real estate operation) conspired with the two lawyers. Jerry Mark was convinced that if this information had been made public during his trial, the jury might have discerned possible motives that might have driven a killer to take revenge on his father.

Here are the highlights of that decision as published:

The court finds that this action arises as the result of the purchase of a 278.5 acre farmed owned partially by Nettie Miller, with a small fraction owned by some distant relatives. Nettie Miller at the time of this transaction was ninety-five years of age and was confined to the Cedar Falls Lutheran Home for the Aged.

...

In August of 1973, Wayne Mark came to the office of W. W. Sindlinger and made an offer for the purchase of the Nettie Miller Property. This offer was for the sum of $140,000 or a per acre value of approximately $500. In conveyance this offer to Audrey Zeiger [the aged niece of Nettie Miller] W. W. Sindlinger suggested to her that she should seriously consider this offer as it could well be in everyone's interest, particularly Nettie's, to get the farm sold so that proceeds would produce adequate income to take care of her.

It must be noted that he did not suggest raising the cash rent [which was $11.00 an acre per year from the man whom she had hired to live on the property and run the farm some 31 years earlier]. It was at this time that Audrey Zeiger indicated that she did not wish to deal with Wayne Mark because he had been trying to buy the farm for years from Nettie but that he had never offered a fair price, but did agree to discuss with W.W. Sindlinger the possible sale of the property.

...

In May of 1975, Wayne Mark was in the office of W.W. Sindlinger and on this occasion he suggested the possibility of Wayne Mark, W.W. Sindlinger and the defendant, Leo M. Baker, buying the Nettie Miller farm. The defendant was asked if he cared to participate, and he readily agreed.

It was decided that they should make an offer of $200,000, and, in order to overcome the problem with the sale of the property to Wayne Mark, they decided to use a nominee to serve as the purchaser. At this time the defendant agreed to participate, apparently without any discussion of what farm or the circumstances of the purchase; but W.W. Sindlinger did suggest to the defendant that it would be necessary to obtain a nominee because the seller would not deal with Wayne Mark.

...

The state has proven fraud on the basis of three separate misrepresentations (1) a misrepresentation as to the true identity of the purchasers of the property. (2) a misrepresentation as to the value of the property and the price which it could be sold for; (3) a misrepresentation as to the need to sell the property.

As to the true identity of the purchasers of the property is without dispute that W.W. Sindlinger misrepresented to Audrey Zeiger that the purchase of the property was Richard Doerfer, when the purchasers were in fact W.W. Sindlinger, Wayne Mark, and the Defendant. Further, by the very nature of the representation, W.W. Sindlinger has to know it was false.

Finally, this representation was clearly material, as Audrey Zeiger would not have sold the property to Wayne Mark under any circumstances...

...

When the sale was completed, W.W. Sindlinger and defendant made an instant profit which in reality belonged to the estate and the heirs of Nettie Miller. Not only did the misrepresentations about value induce Audrey to sell for less money than she wanted to, the misrepresentations as to identity of purchasers [Wayne Mark in particular] induced her to sell when she would not have sold at all.

(Waterloo *Courier*, July 30, 1978, p. 10.)

CONCLUSION

Many aspects of this story still puzzle me to the point of wonderment. When so few complicated plans work out as planned, why did so much of Jerry Mark's motorcycle trip go exactly right for him? Why didn't he get a ticket, or a flat tire, or dump the Honda and have to get it repaired, delaying him for days and making his plans moot? Why was he able to ride all but nonstop for so many hours with terrible tailbone pain? Why didn't he have second thoughts along the way and call it off, given all the trouble it caused him? A toxic combination of white-hot anger, arrogance, revenge, jealousy, and (possibly) greed seemed to drive him on, and everything had to go perfectly for days for him to commit those murders.

Then after the murders everything seemed to go utterly wrong, predictably enough. Investigators were able to find several eyewitnesses who placed him much nearer the crime scene than he ever admitted. Within a few days they even found the source of those odd .38 Long Colt cartridges, sold to him by a clerk from Waterloo, Iowa. The phone companies' (there were more than one) records were about to be destroyed when investigators subpoenaed them and begin the tedious work of pouring through them all—and finding exactly which calls were made, from where, and when—on pay phones, no less.

David Dutton told me more than once that the judge Carroll Engelkes (and Dutton agreed) felt that the hand of the Almighty was with them during the investigation. But where was the Almighty during that grueling three-day, nearly 2,000 mile ride? With Jerry? I have not been able to reconcile the Almighty's hand so much as plain, dumb bad luck for the Leslie Mark family, then just as bad luck for Jerry. And I'm still in awe of the quality of the investigation and prosecution, thanks to both Tom Ruxlow and David Dutton's teams of policeman, highway patrolmen, detectives, and lawyers.

Three aspects of this story stand out most for me now.

(1) The mind of a sociopath.

I've become convinced that Jerry Mark is a classic sociopath, a man without a conscience, and he was probably born that way. His ethic was simple: whatever he could get by with. History is replete with people without scruples, who will do anything to get what they want, who spend their lives blaming others while seeking gratification of their every desire. Sometimes they do no real harm, but sometimes they inflict the most awful burdens on everyone around them—and continue to blame everyone but themselves. That's the Jerry Mark I've come to know through my research and in writing this account.

(2) The terrible aftermath.

I've spent much time talking with the living victims of this crime, including Jerry's mother Dorothy (now deceased) and George and Margaret Colthurst, whose "victim's impact" statement ends this book. When their son and daughter and grandchildren were murdered their lives were turned upside down in every conceivable way. They experienced grief and trauma beyond imagining, and each family dealt with it entirely differently. Dorothy defended and stood by Jerry until she died at 91 in 2009. She lived with a certainty that Jerry would someday be found innocent, though I believe she was never quite convinced. During our long interview, she admitted that she struggled with her second eldest son, wondering at times what in the world he had been thinking when he bought and signed for those cartridges, then lied to the police about it. Because she was called as a defense witness, she never heard the full evidence as Dutton presented it in the trial. She did experience a few weeks of vindication over Judge O'Brien's decision in 2006, convinced that Jerry was about to be exonerated. Justice at last, she must have thought.

The Colthursts, in contrast, felt almost immediately that something was wrong about Jerry's story. He was nowhere to be found when the murders occurred, and a revolver had disappeared. When he did show up at the Mark home in Cedar Falls, just before the funeral, his story seemed unbelievable, too coincidental with the crime to be credible. And when he was arrested, then released on parole, Jerry absolutely refused to talk to either of them, even though at least once he had the opportunity. To the Colthursts, his avoidance behavior after his arrest confirmed their worst suspicion: the police had their man, their son-in-law's brother.

As the Colthursts have said many times, a day never passes that they don't wish Jerry would have been executed, partly for their own peace of mind, and partly because having their own daughter killed and her killer kept alive by the state seems a monstrous injustice.

(3) The meaning of it all.

As I've finished this book I've been teaching the films of Alfred Hitchcock to a class of undergraduates. Hitchcock was a brave film-maker who undertook to examine what most of us deny: that at any time, our happy, "normal" lives can be destroyed or changed in ways we can't anticipate or even imagine. Hitchcock fought complacency, and realized on the deepest level that all humans are at the mercy of forces beyond their control. Premeditated murder was his favorite subject, often based on stories taken from real events. Hitchcock draws the same conclusion in film after film: even the most successful, productive, and "safe" lives can be ended brutally and violently at any time.

Under the right circumstances, even by a once-beloved brother.

The Colthursts' Victims' Impact Statement
George and Margaret Colthurst, parents of Jorjean Mark,
Grandparents of Julie and Jeffrey Mark
March 2011

Note: When Jerry Mark was convicted in 1976, the state of Iowa was years away from victims' restitution or impact statement laws. Accordingly, the Colthursts were never given a chance to make their feelings known about the murders and the murderer.

I asked them to write their own comment for this book, and they used the opportunity to write the victims' impact statement they would have made at the time.

Some of it is addressed directly to Jerry Mark, as it would have been had they read it in court at his sentencing.

All that we have left are the memories of a vibrant, thriving young family. Les and Jorjean Mark, both 25, Julie Julane, age five, and Jeffrey Wayne Mark, age 21 months.

Leslie Mark was an aggressive and good farm manager. He was voted Outstanding Farmer of the Year in Blackhawk County. He was a great dad to his children and a loving husband to his wife.

Jorjean was our only daughter. She was kind, energetic, had a bubbly spirit, and was always trying to help someone. She was a wonderful mother to their children. When she and Les married, she plunged into the farming operation with all her drive and energy. She did all she could to help Les in his work and to provide a warm, loving environment for their children to grow up in. Their home was a busy, happy place.

Three weeks before they were murdered, Margaret and I came up to their home to help them pack up for their move to the home farm. Les was away helping his dad and the children were upstairs taking a nap.

Jorjean, Margaret, and I were in the kitchen emptying cupboards into boxes for the move. We took a short break as we visited. I said to Jorjean, "Honey, you have no idea how many times a day we think of you and Les, and your little family. We try to think of an excuse to come up and see you again. We just want you to know that you are all and more that we could ever ask for in a daughter. We love you so very much."

Three weeks later she was gone. All we have are memories of our much-loved young family.

Jerry Alan Mark. You are a murderer. Consumed by jealousy, envy, and greed, you killed a family of four, execution style. You shot your brother Les 5 times. You were best man at their wedding. You shot his wife Jorjean 4 times. You shot your niece Julie, a beautiful little 5-year-old girl in the heart and again in the right eye in her bed. You shot little Jeff, your nephew, in the heart and in the eye while he was sleeping.

Jerry, you are a habitual liar. You lied to the police, the detectives, your parents, your in-laws, your attorneys, and the judges who presided over your trial as well as the 12 jurors who convicted you. You fooled no one.

As David Dutton, prosecuting attorney said, "If you are innocent, Jerry, why all the lies?"

Jerry, you are also a thief. You stole their lives from all four of them, and from us.

You stole our privilege of being able to watch our grandchildren grow up and enjoy the many activities that they would have participated in. You stole all of the future family get-togethers, the Christmas celebrations, the birthdays and Thanksgivings that we would have enjoyed had they lived.

As Margaret said, "We mourn for what might have been."

Jerry Mark, you are the lowest of the scum of the earth. You are a poisonous snake in the family midst. You should have been hung the day after your trial. The world would have been a better place if you had never been born.

Someday you will stand in the highest court there is before the Lord God Almighty to be judged. From that court, there are no appeals.

Our family will never recover from the sorrow and grief you inflicted upon us.

(signed)

George and Margaret Colthurst

Acknowledgments

Within five years of Jerry Mark's conviction in 1976, driven by curiosity and wonder, I began to actively investigate the case, and (with Linda Kettner) interviewed Jerry himself, his mother Dorothy, Jorjean's parents, George and Margaret Colthurst, David Dutton, Lawrence Scalise, and a host of others who knew the case in varying degrees of intimacy. I thank them all for their input, and for the many readers who read and commented on the variety of incarnations this manuscript has undergone: Mark Baldwin, Russell Barrett, John Bresland, Nikki Clasby, Don Charnetski, David Correll, George and Margaret Colthurst, Mike and Cherie Dargan, David Dutton, Sandra Fowler, Mary Edna Fraser, Jim Gritzner, Jack Hovelson, Kris Knebel, Tom Langlas, Loree Rackstraw, Tom Ruxlow, Ron Sandvik, Saul Shapiro, and others that I asked to read and comment on brief passages. All graciously agreed, and all helped shape my thinking and ideas in a variety of necessary and helpful ways. In addition, at the very beginning, Cedar Falls *Record* reporter Linda Kettner helped with the major interviews; in the summer of 1980 we traveled to Fort Madison, Des Moines, and Ainsworth, taping a few interviews and conducting many more. Transcriptions of those interviews were of inestimable value as sources, and I thank Linda for her considerable interviewing skills and enthusiasm, which gave this project a solid grounding.

Finally, I thank those many people who kept asking—with growing impatience—when I was going to finish "that Mark book." After awhile, I felt obliged to bring it all together in this hybrid form, much more nonfiction than fiction, more compelling than a report, but without the soaring imaginative flights of pure fiction. I trust those readers will feel *Brother's Blood* was worth the wait.

Scott Cawelti was born and raised in Cedar Falls, Iowa. He attended the University of Northern Iowa (UNI), graduating with a vocal music education degree in 1965 and a Master's Degree in English in 1968, and a PhD in Modern Letters from the University of Iowa in 1978. Dr. Cawelti taught at UNI from 1968-2008 and continues to teach a variety of courses as an adjunct since his retirement. He has published two writing textbooks and edited *The Complete Poetry of James Hearst, (University of Iowa, 2001)*. In December, 2010, he released a CD, *Landscape Iowa, 16 James Hearst Poems, Sung* in which he performs (with twelve other musicians) James Hearst poems he set to music.

He is married to Dr. Angeleita Floyd, Professor of Music (flute) at the University of Northern Iowa, and has two children and four grandchildren.